Altea Gallery
Catalogue No 4
Summer 2017

Cartouches, Creatures & Caricature: Decoration on maps

Introduction

The items in this catalogue have been chosen as exemplars of the mapmaker's art, demonstrating the various devices used to embellish their work, turning information into art.

The selection is purposely diverse, attempting to illustrate the evolution of both style and technique, with items from six different centuries.

THE THEATRUM ORBIS TERRARUM

The Theatrum is regarded as the first modern atlas, i.e. a comprehensive series of maps drawn in a standard format rather than being a collection of various maps. It set the standard for decoration on maps for the period, with strapwork cartouches, galleons and monsters, expertly engraved by Frans Hogenberg. In the introduction to the first edition of 1570 Ortelius wrote of his debt to 'the artful hands of Frans Hogenberg, by whose untiring diligence nearly all these plates were engraved'. It was highly-paid work: shortly after the completion of the Theatrum Hogenberg could afford to open his own studio in Cologne and embark on the equally ambitious city atlas, the six-volume 'Civitatis Orbis Terrarum'.

The first German edition of Ortelius's atlas

1   ORTELIUS, Abraham.

Theatrum oder Schawplatz des erdbodems, warin die Landttafell der gantzen weldt, mit sambt aine der selben kurtze erklarng zu sehen ist. Durch Abrahamum Ortelium.

Antwerp: Gielis von Diest for the Author, 1572, German text edition. Large 2°, C17th mottled calf gilt, rebacked with original spine laid on, marbled edges; pp. (xii), titlepage with German title label pasted over the original Latin; 53 maps in fine original colour + (6) (epilogue & Index, privilege & colophon). Damp staining affecting up to map 3, with restoration to the margins of the first two maps; pair of worm holes affecting to map 12, a few filled; a few other small repairs.

This first German edition of the Theatrum, published only two years after the first, still contained only the original 53 maps: the world & four continents, 30 maps of regions of Europe and eight of the rest of the world.

This example is on particularly good-quality paper, allowing it to withstand the effects of the original green colour well.

VAN DEN BROECKE: p.24, estimating 150 copies printed; KOEMAN: Ort 5.

S/N **16742**

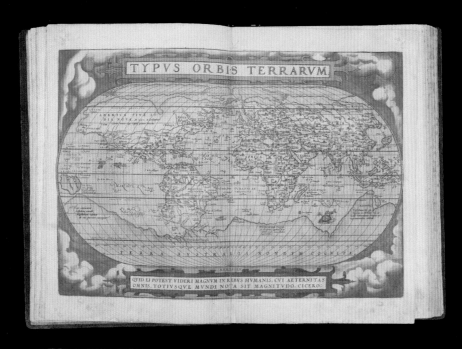

The year after this German edition the first 'Additamentum' was issued, containing 16 new maps. Eventually the number of maps in the 'Theatrum' reached 166, as new surveys were sent to Ortelius for appraisal. It is a mark of Ortelius's scholarly approach that he was careful to credit his sources. Below are four maps not in the original edition of the 'Theatrum', but regarded as landmark maps.

Ortelius's landmark map of China in fine original colour

2   ORTELIUS, Abraham.

Chinae, olim Sinarum regionis, nova descriptio. auctore Ludovicio Georgio.

Antwerp: Jan Baptist Vrients, 1603, Latin text edition. Fine original colour. 370 x 470mm. Verdigris crack in unprinted area of map repaired; text trimmed on verso with edges reinforced with archivist's tissue.

The most decorative map of China: oriented with north to the right, there are cartouches for the title, scale and privilege; on the map are elephants, Tartar tents and land-yachts. Japan has an extra landmass to the east, with its further reaches hidden by the scale cartouche. The Philippines appear, but with little accuracy or detail; they were not even named until the second state (c.1588).

WALTER: 11f, illus; VAN DEN BROECKE: 164.

S/N **17444**

A 16th century map of the unknown North Pacific

3   ORTELIUS, Abraham.

Tartariae Sive Magni Chami Regni typus.

Antwerp, 1598, French text edition. Coloured. 360 x 490mm.

A fine map of Tartary, showing from the Black Sea to the North Pacific, with an out-sized Japan and a peninsular California. It is decorated with strapwork cartouches for the title and scale, vignettes of the Tsar and the Grand Cham sitting before tents, and galleons & flying fish.

Of interest is the depiction of the Strait of Anian, a narrow stretch of water dividing America and Asia, believed to be an easy way to reach the riches of Cathay. On the Asian side is 'Argon', which was, according to the engraved text, a former Christian kingdom known to Prester John of Africa.

VAN DEN BROECKE: 163; WALTER: 11e.

S/N **14889**

The first map of the Pacific, in superb original colour

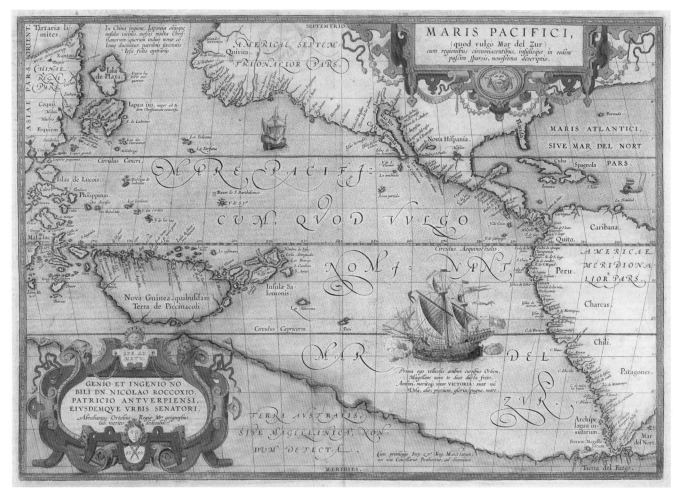

4   ORTELIUS, Abraham.

Maris Pacifici, (quod vulgo Mar del Zur) cum regionibus circumiacentibus, insulusque in eodem passim sparsis, novissima descriptio.

Antwerp, 1608 or 1612, Italian text edition. Fine original colour. 345 x 495mm.

One of Ortelius's most popular maps, depicting the Pacific and most of the Americas. Engraved in 1589, it predates the concept of California as an island, has a huge island of New Guinea and an unrecognisable Japan. The south Pacific is filled with a vignette of the 'Victoria', Magellan's ship: his route through the Magellan Straits is shown, with Terra del Fuego depicted as part of the huge 'Terra Australis'.

VAN DEN BROECKE: 12.

S/N **13661**

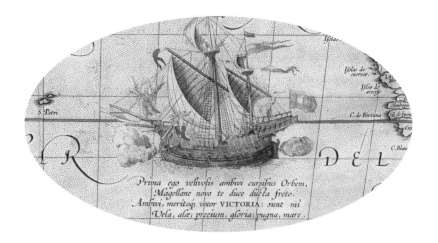

Vrients's scarce map of England, Wales & Ireland

5 VRIENTS, Jan Baptist.

Angliae et Hiberniae Accurata Descriptio... 1605.

Antwerp: Plantin, 1609 or 1612, Latin text edition. Coloured. 435 x 570mm. Slightly trimmed at sides due to the width of the map, new margins.

A map of England, Wales & Ireland, published to commemorate the ascendency of James VI of Scotland to the English throne in 1603, as James I. It is decorated with his family tree, armorials and vignettes including Neptune on a sea-horse. This example is from the second state, with the controversial description of James I as king of France removed.

This map was only added to the 'Theatrum' after the death of Ortelius, when Vrients bought the rights to the atlas. Already some of the maps were showing signs of age, both physically and stylistically, so Vrients added several new maps, with decorations of a more contemporary taste. As this map only appears in the later editions of the 'Theatrum' it is comparatively rare: Van den Broecke estimates that only about 1,250 were printed. Shirley notes that because the map is larger than the standard Ortelius maps it is 'often found with damage to the margins'.

SHIRLEY: 323 & 275 for main description, 'an exceptionally fine map'.

S/N **15776**

15 OUTSTANDING WORLD MAPS

The first map in an atlas was usually of the world, so it was important for making that vital first impression. Subsequently much more effort was made to make it the most ornate of the series, filling the borders with illustrations, both informative and allegorical.

Below are fifteen maps on various projections, illustrating the development of style from the 17th century.

The most decorative Ptolemaic world map

6 MERCATOR, Gerard.

Universalis Tabula Iuxta Ptolemæum.

Amsterdam: Jodocus Hondius Jnr, 1618. Fine original colour. 350 x 490mm.

A map of the world according to Claudius Ptolemy of Alexandria, showing the world as known to the ancients, with the semi-mythical island of Taprobana but no America or Cape of Good Hope. However Mercator has dropped the land-locked Indian Ocean shown on earlier Ptolemaic maps.

The map was engraved by Mercator himself for his 1578 edition of Ptolemy's 'Geography'; however this example comes from an edition of Petrus Bertius's 'Theatrum geographiae veteris'.

The flamboyance of the strapwork-and-windhead borders makes this map the most decorative of the Ptolemaic world maps.

SHIRLEY: World 139, plate 118, 'His general Ptolemaic map is one of the finest available... elegantly engraved'.

S/N **16747**

'A fine ornate example of the decorative cartography of the time'

7 HONDIUS, Henricus.

Nova Totius Terrarum Orbis Geographica Ac Hydrographica Tabula. Auct Henr. Hondio.

Amsterdam: Jan Jansson, 1641-, Latin text edition. Fine original colour. 380 x 540mm. Minor repairs on verso to verdigris weaknesses.

A striking example of the first world map to appear in an atlas showing California as an island and, according to Schiller, 'the oldest dated map in an atlas on which a Dutch discovery in Australia has been shown'. The Cape York Peninsula is shown with eight names.

The decoration on the map is superb: three strapwork cartouches appear on the map; portraits of Julius Cæsar, Ptolemy, Mercator and Jodocus Hondius fill the corners; scenes representing the four Elements are above and below each hemisphere; in the upper cusp is a celestial globe; and in the lower cusp are allegorical figures representing Asia, America and Africa making obeisance to Europe.

KOEMAN: 51A; SCHILDER: Australia Unveiled, 39; SHIRLEY: 336, 'a fine ornate example of the decorative cartography of the time'.

S/N **16889**

A Dutch world map with superb decorative borders

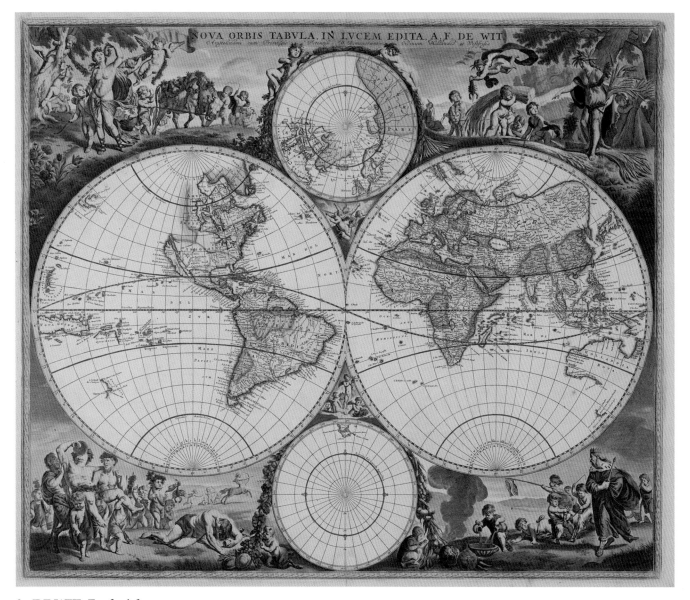

8 DE WIT, Frederick.

Nova Orbis Tabula in Lucem Edita.

Amsterdam, 1675. Original colour. 465 x 540mm. Minor reinforcements to verdigris cracks on verso

An exquisite seventeenth century map of the world in double-hemisphere, with two further spheres showing the northern and southern hemispheres and cherubs in the cusps. The four corners are taken up with vignettes of the seasons, each with references to the Elements and the Zodiac.

The first state of the map was issued c.1670, but the cherubs in the cusps and the engraved border mark this as the second state. Another plate replaced it in 1680.

SHIRLEY: World 451 - 'one of the most attractive of its time... one of the finest that is relatively easily obtainable by the map collector'.

S/N **17451**

Joannes Blaeu's double-hemisphere world map with superior colour

9 BLAEU, Johannes.

Nova et Accuratissima Totius Terrarum Orbis Tabula.

Amsterdam, 1662, Latin text edition. Exceptional original colour, with gold and silver highlights. 415 x 540mm. Minor repair to split in centre fold in lower margin.

The new double-hemisphere world map, drawn up by Johannes Blaeu to replace the map first issued by his father Willem in 1606 and used in their atlases from 1630. The quality of the original colour suggests it was coloured by one of the most famous Dutch colourists, Dirk Janszoon van Santen.

This new map is a great departure in style, being double-hemisphere rather than on the former's Mercator Projection. Above the map are allegorical figures of the planets, the sun & moon, with two cartographers at the sides. Underneath are allegorical figures of the Four Seasons, each drawn by either birds or animals. The cartography is much improved, with the removal of the Great Southern Continent and the addition of the pre-Cook outlines of Australia and New Zealand. Unfortunately Blaeu has chosen to show California as an island, dropping the peninsular depiction of his father.

This example comes from the first issue of the 'Atlas Major', the first atlas to contain this map.

SHIRLEY: World 428.

S/N **16806**

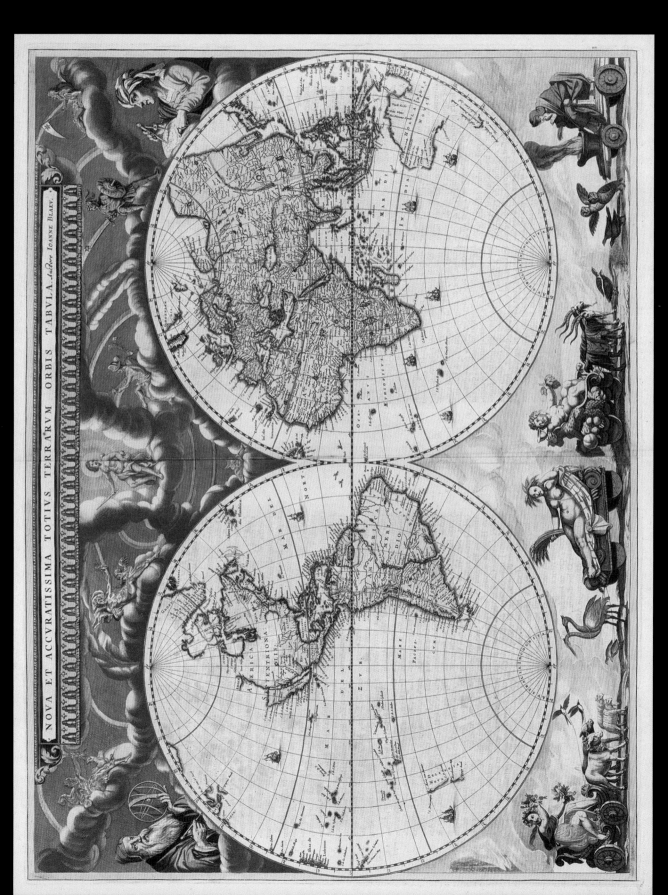

A world map with portraits of the Twelve Cæsars

10   VISSCHER, Claes Janszoon.

Nova Totius Terrarum Orbis Geographica ac Hydrographica Tabula.

Amsterdam, 1652. Original colour. 445 x 560mm. Restoration to margin and centre fold.

This magnificent planisphere manages to include 30 separate illustrations in its panels. Along the top and bottom are equestrian portraits of the Twelve Cæsars of Tacitus. The four corners feature female allegorical figures of the Continents, with Europe as a shepherdess, Asia seated on a camel, Africa on a crocodile and America on an armadillo! The left border has prospects of Rome, Amsterdam, Jerusalem and Tunis, interspersed with illustrations of European, Asian and African dress. The right border is given over completely to America: the prospects of Mexico City, Havana, Pernambuco and Todos os Santos Bay are separated by vignettes of North American natives, South Americans and the giants of the Magellan Strait.

Originally published in 1639, most of the cartography has been copied from Blaeu, although Arctic America has been extended, as has the St Lawrence River. This state has the date 1652, the year of Visscher's death.

SHIRLEY: 350.

S/N **17720**

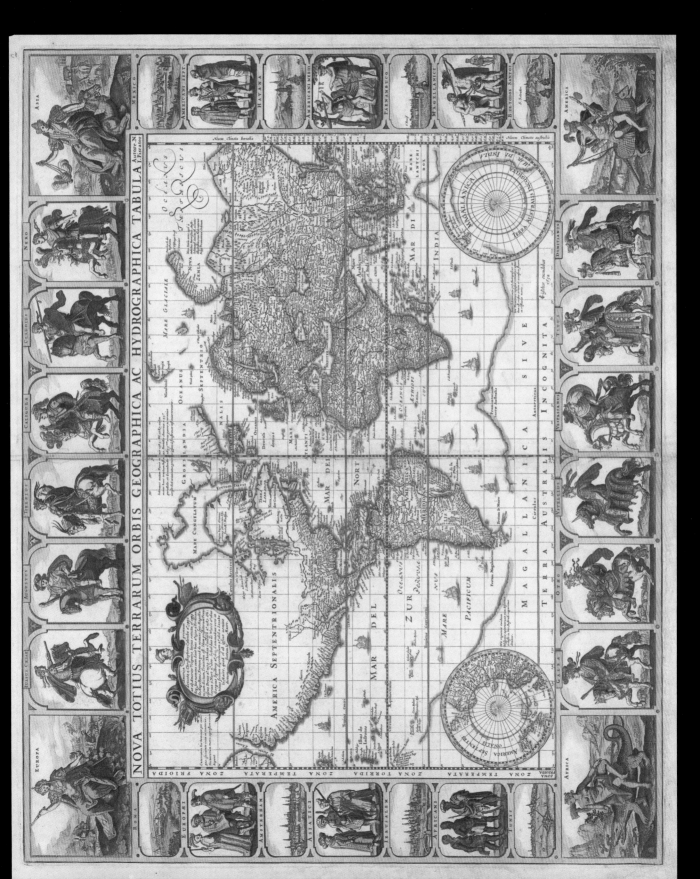

A lavishly-decorated 17th century double-hemisphere world map

11   DANCKERTS, Justus.

Nova Totius Terrarum Orbis Tabula.

Amsterdam, c.1685. Original colour. 490 x 590mm.

A double-hemisphere world with two polar spheres in the cusps. California is an island; the islands of 'Jedso' and 'Terre Esonis' in the north Pacific; and Australia and New Zealand are only partial outlines.

The allegorical scenes in the corners feature the Four Elements: 'Earth' is represented by farming; 'Air' by birds, classical figures for the bodies of the Solar System, with signs of the Zodiac; 'Fire' by war, with a battle scene with a burning city; and 'Water' has trading ships, mer-people and a whale.

SHIRLEY: 529.

S/N **17538**

A highly decorative pair of hemispheres

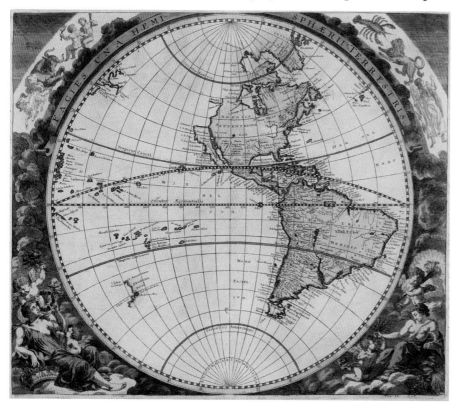

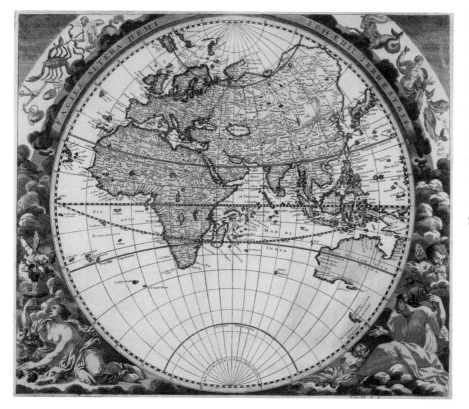

12   ZAHN, Johann.

Facies Una Hemisphærii Terrestris.;
Facies Altera Hemisphærii
Terrestris.

*Nuremberg, c.1696, coloured, each 360
x 415mm. Centre folds restored.*

This fine pair of hemispheres were
published in Zahn's 'Mundus
Mirabili'. The geography is based
on traditional Dutch maps of the
1660's and shows such anomalies as
California as an island, Australia
with an incomplete coastline and
joined to Papua New Guinea and
New Zealand denoted by only one
coast. Also shown is the Strait of
Anian which was thought to
connect Siberia and Alaska. The
borders of each map depict the
seasons as classical figures and the
signs of the Zodiac.

Johann Zahn (1631-1707) was a
philosopher of the
Præmonstratensian order in
Würtzburg, who wrote a number of
pseudo-scientific works
accompanied by engravings of the
highest standard. His work was
produced during a period of history
known as the 'Enlightenment'
when scientific experimentation
and philosophical debate were
encouraged by a European nobility
hungry for new knowledge.

SHIRLEY 584 illus.

S/N **9684**

An English world map after the Longitude Act

13   SENEX, John.

A New Map of the World From the Latest Observations. Revis'd by I.Senex. Most humbly Inscribd to his Royal Highness George Prince of Wales.

London, c.1720. Original outline colour with additions to the borders. 430 x 550mm.

An elegantly engraved double-hemisphere map of the world with four further spheres on different projections, an armillary sphere flanked by two figures (one being Hercules) and allegorical figures of the four continents around the title.

On the map California is an island (although not on two of the smaller spheres), 'Jesso' is joined to mainland Asia, and Australia is joined to New Guinea via Carpentaria.

Unusual features on this map are the faint outlines offering alternative coastlines around the countries furthest from Europe. The Longitude Act of 1714, in which a prize of £20,000 was offered for an accurate method of measuring longitude at sea, highlighted the fact that the exact locations of countries on the other side of the world had yet to be determined. This map displays an unusual admission of lack of certainty by a cartographer!

Although this example is marked 'Revis'd' we have been unable to trace an earlier version. George was made Prince of Wales in 1714, and came to the throne of England in 1727 as George II.

S/N **17314**

Jacques Cassini's planisphere with superb decoration

14   AA, Pieter van der.

Planisphere Terrestre Suivant les nouvelles Observations des Astronomes Dressé et presenté au Roy tres Chretien par Mr. Cassini le Fils, de l'Academie Royal des Sciences.

Leiden: van der Aa, 1713. Coloured, 550 x 665mm. Narrow top margin.

A close copy of Jacques Cassini's extremely rare map published by Nolin in 1696, showing the world on an Azimuthal equidistant projection (i.e. in a single sphere, centred on the North Pole, heavily distorting the Antipodes). This, in turn, was based on Jean-Dominique Cassini's 8-metre map prepared for the French Academy of Sciences in the 1680s, the first map to set standard longitudes for known places based on the observations of the moons of Jupiter. Here the sites where the readings were taken are marked with stars.

In the Cassini-Nolin map the corners were left blank; here they have been embellished with designs by Jan Goree, with four large classical figures, including Mercury, cherubs and the signs of the Zodiac. On the map California is an island.

See SHIRLEY 579 for Cassini's original.

S/N **17611**

A German double-hemisphere world map

15   SEUTTER, Matthäus.

Diversi Globi Terr-Aquei...

Augsburg, c.1730. Original colour. 510 x 590mm.

A fine double-hemisphere world map, with eight further hemispheres showing the Earth from different angles, surrounded by the allegorical wind-heads. California appears as an island; Ezo is a large adjunct to Japan, with 'Campangie Land' just to the north; and Australia and New Zealand are partial outlines.

S/N **17037**

A mid-18th century world map full of false assumptions

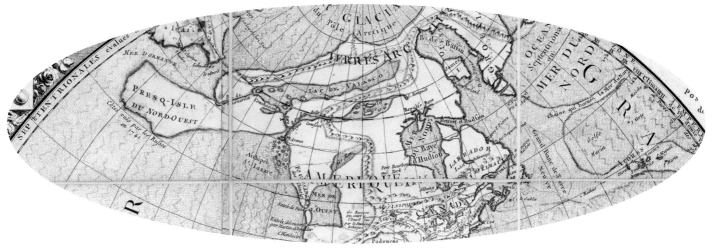

16   DENIS, Louis.

Mappe-monde Physique Politique et Mathematique ou Nouvelle Maniere de considerer la Terre par la Disposition naturelle de ses parties par les differents Peuples qui l'habitant et par sa Correspondance avec le Ciel. Extraite des cartes des S.rs de Cassini, Danville, De l'Isle, Bellin et autres géographes.

Paris: Denis, 1764. Original colour. Three sheets conjoined, dissected and laid on linen as issued, total 640 x 1275mm.

A double-hemisphere world map with the Americas in the right sphere, a decorative title cartouche, a world map is a single sphere in the lower cusp and geographical diagrams in the four corners.

What makes this map so fascinating is the amount of cartographical conjecture: at the Poles are various islands, including a huge one incorporating New Zealand; Australia's east coastline reaches Vanutu; in North America are the Mer de l'Ouest, Lac de Fonte and a large island instead of Alaska; in Africa a chain of mountains stretches across Guinea, thirty years before James Rennell was accused of inventing the 'Mountains of Kong'.

Although not listed in the list of sources, much of the information comes from Philippe Buache, 'Premier Géographe du Roi' from 1729. He believed that the mountains of the world were linked, crossing the ocean floors from continent to continent, most noticeably across the Pacific.

BAYNTON-WILLIAMS: New Worlds, p.171-3.

S/N **16190**

Brion's magnificent large-format map of the world

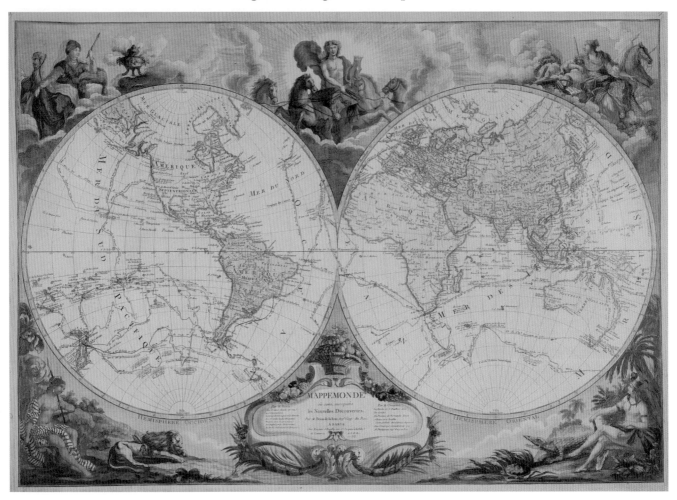

17   BRION DE LA TOUR, Louis.

Mappemonde où sont marquées les Nouvelles Découvertes.

Paris: Esnauts & Rapilly, 1783. Coloured. 530 x 765mm.

A double-hemisphere world map with the Americas in the right sphere, a decorative title cartouche and a world map is a single sphere in the two cusps, and geographical diagrams in the four corners.

S/N **15691**

Georgian two-sheet double-hemisphere map of the world

18   THOMPSON, George.

A New Map of the World with all the New Discoveries, By Cap:t Cook & other Navigators Including the Trade Winds, Monsoons and Variations of the Compass, Illustrated with a Coelestial Planisphere, the Various Systems of Ptolomy, Copernicus & Tycho Bray, Together with the Appearences of the Planets &c.

London: G. Thompson, 1798. Original colour. Two sheets conjoined, total 630 x 950mm.

A double-hemisphere map of the world at the end of the 18th century, surrounded by insets of polar and other projections, celestial spheres in the cusps and other astronomical diagrams.

George Thompson (1758-1826) was a very successful London publisher, despite most of his output being derivative; he left an estate worth £70,000 although this was much reduced by the legal wrangles over the will that lasted until at least 1834.

ARMITAGE: The World at Their Fingertips, Map 23.

S/N **13897**

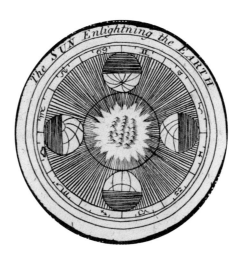

Very decorative 19th century map of the world

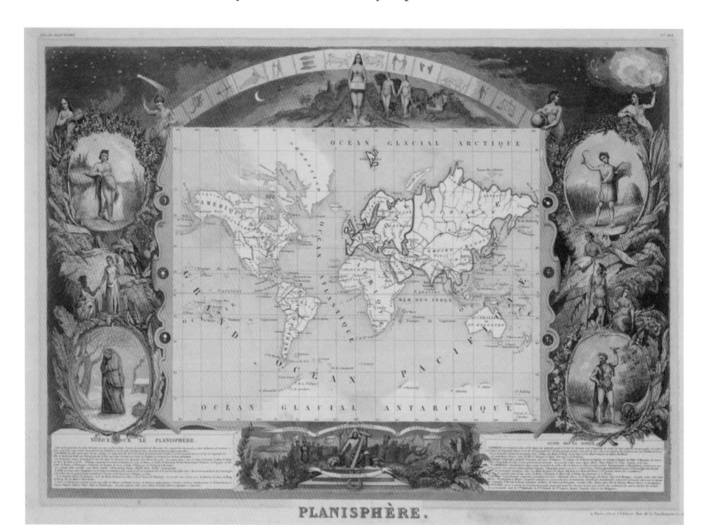

19 LEVASSEUR, Victor.

Planisphère.

Paris: Pelissier, c.1845. Outline colour. 310 x 410mm.

A fine map of the world on Mercator's projection, with ornate engraved borders, medallion allegories of the Four Seasons and vignettes of gods, goddesses, mythical figures, Adam and Eve, astrological symbols and animals. Under the map is a further vingette with Jesus seated on a throne with a cross in one hand. Around him can be seen Napoleon, Socrates, pyramids and a herm.

It was published in one of the last decorative atlases, the 'Atlas Universel Illustré'.

S/N **17822**

A vivid poster map of the GPO's mail routes

20 GILL, Leslie MacDonald.

Mail Steamship Routes.

Portsmouth: General Post Office, 1937. Colour lithograph, 990 x 1230mm. A few small signs of wear, mounted on linen.

A colourful map of the world, on an azimuthal projection although Gill has chosen to depict two Antarcticas (one under Australia, the other under South America) rather than stretch the ice out across the bottom of the map. In the top corners are illustrations of a post box, a postal van and the loading of the mail onto a steamship. Under the map are eleven roundel depictions of the development of ocean-going craft, from the time of the Vikings, through the Middle Ages to East Indiamen, Brunel's 'Great Eastern' of 1858 and RMS 'Queen Mary' (now moored at Long Beach). Either side of the title is the new logo of the GPO, also designed by Gill.

Leslie MacDonald Gill (1884-1947, known as Max), younger brother of Eric Gill, specialised in graphic design in the Arts and Crafts style. His most important commission was from the Imperial War Graves Commission, designing the script used on Commission headstones and war memorials, including the 'Thiepval Memorial to the Missing of the Somme'. His 'Wonderground Map of London', originally drawn as an advertising poster for London Electric Underground Railway Company in 1914, was such a success it is credited with saving the 'UndergrounD' advertising campaign.

S/N **17396**

CARTE-À-FIGURE MAPS

Carte-à-figure maps were popularised in the first part of the seventeenth century and are the most recognisable genres in map design, with city prospects and illustrations of local dress in panels.

Speed's classic carte-à-figure maps of the Continents

Four Maps from John Speed's 'Prospect of the Most Famous Parts of the World', the first English atlas of the World.

21 Europ, and the Cheife Cities Contained therein Described; with the Habits of Most Kingdoms Now in Use. By Jo: Speed. Ano: Dom: 1626.

London: Bassett & Chiswell, 1676. Coloured. 390 x 510mm.

A classic decorative map of Europe, with ten costume vignettes down the sides and eight city prospects, including London, Rome & Venice, along the top.

Of interest is the continued presence of the mythical island of Frisland, south west of Iceland.

S/N **13726**

22 Asia with the Islands Adioyning described, the atire of the people & Townes of importance, all of them newly augmented by J:S: Ano. Dom: 1626.

London: Bassett & Chiswell, 1676. Coloured. 390 x 510mm.

The first map of Asia by an Englishman (although Speed still had to turn to a Dutch engraver, Abraham Goos, to produce it), first published 1627.

Down the sides are ten costume vignettes, and eight city prospects, including Jerusalem, Goa and Macao, run along the top of the map. On verso is an English text, 'The Description of Asia', containing a mixture of fact and amusing myth.

S/N **17816**

23 America with those known parts in that unknowne worlde, both people and manner of buildings Discribed and inlarged by J.S. 1626.

London: Bassett & Chiswell, 1676. Coloured. 405 x 525mm. Repaired tear entering printed border top left.

A landmark map of America, being the first atlas map to show California is an island, engraved by Abraham Goos. Above California is the outline of another large, unnamed island; nothing is shown of the Great Lakes; and Raleigh's 'Parime Lacus' and 'Manoa' appear in South America. An inset shows Greenland, Iceland and the mythical island of Frisland.

Originally published in 1627, the plate was altered in the 1660s to add English place names including Boston, 'Long Ile', 'Mary Land' and Carolina.

Along the top of the map are prospects of eight cities, including Havana, Cartagena, Mexico City and Rio de Janeiro. Down the sides are ten costume vignettes of native Americans, including the kings of New England & Florida, a Virginian and Greenlander.

BURDEN: North America, 217.

S/N **17815**

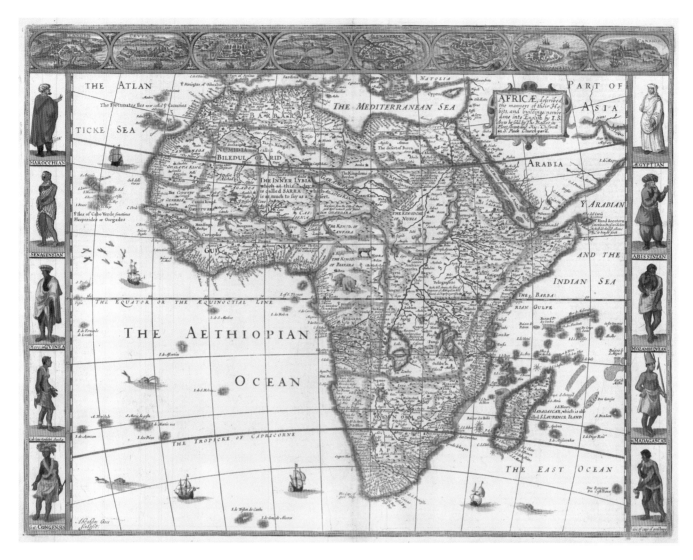

24   Africæ, described, the manners of their habits, and buildinge: newly done into English by J.S.

London: Bassett & Chiswell, 1676. Coloured. 405 x 525mm. Repairs in margins of bottom corners.

Along the top of the map are prospects of eight cities, including Alexandria, Cairo, Tunis and Algiers. Down the sides are ten costume vignettes of African natives, including an Egyptian, Abyssinian Madagascan and a man from the Cape of Good Hope.

BETZ: Africa, 62, state 3.

S/N **17814**

Unrecorded carte-à-figures map of Asia

25   SABATINI, Francesco.

Asia Recens Summa Cura Delineata...

Bologna: Sabatini, 1670, 455 x 555mm Bottom right corner rebuilt with manuscript reinstatement, otherwise a very fine example.

A very rare and attractive carte-à-figures map of Asia, engraved by Pietro Todeschi. The side panels contain native costume figures and miniature vignette views of major towns and cities, amongst which are shown Goa, Macao and Calcutta. Of interest in the map is the North-Eastern truncation of China/Siberia, presumably due to a belief in a North-West passage through the Straits of Anian.

This map was published by Francesco Sabatini, one of the many fringe figures in Italian map-making and publishing in the late seventeenth century. Unfortunately even accurate dates for his life and death elude us, while his work life can be established only by the rough dating of his maps dependent on the dedications on those maps bearing them, but he was apparently active as a printer and publisher (and possibly engraver) in the 1670s, probably in Bologna.

This is a contemporary piracy of Dutch carte-à-figures maps, popularised in the first part of the seventeenth century, although it seems likely that the map was plagiarised from intermediate Italian copies, perhaps by Stefano Scolari, an engraver and publisher (or possibly two different men) active from the 1640s to 1660s.

STOPP: 'Drie Karten von Francesco Sabatini'; SCHILDER: 'Mappæ Antiquæ Liber Amicorum' p.281-285.

S/N **10576**

Rare English carte-à-figures map of Asia

26 OVERTON, John.

A New Plaine and most Exact map of Asia described by NI Vischer and rendered into English with the habits of the countries and manner of the cheife citties.

London, 1671. Coloured. 425 x 540mm with wide margins.

A scarce panelled map of Asia, featuring ten city prospects, including Jerusalem, Goa, Macao and Aden, eight costume vignettes and six fanciful portraits of Asian kings.

Based on the Visscher issue of Keere's map of 1614, it was originally engraved in 1668; this is an example of the second state, with Overton's new address. Apparently Overton was planning a world atlas and

lacked maps of the continents, so had them engraved. As the matching map of Africa is signed by Philip Holmes the stylistic similarity makes it likely that Holmes also engraved the Asia.

Little of Overton's output was original: he bought the stock of Peter Stent after his death from the plague in 1665, and c.1700 he bought Speed's county map plates.

S/N **9340**

The famous English carte-à-figures map of Tartary

27 SPEED, John.

A Newe Mape of Tartary...

London: Bassett & Chiswell, 1676. Coloured. 395 x 515mm, with wide margins.

A highly decorative map of the Russian Empire, finely engraved by Dirck Gryp for Speed's 'Prospect of the Most Famous Parts of the World', with eight costume vignettes down the sides and four city prospects, including Astrakhan & Samarkand, along the top. On the map the Caspian Sea is still wider than it is tall; the Straits of Anian appear with no sign of Kamchatka; and Korea is an island.

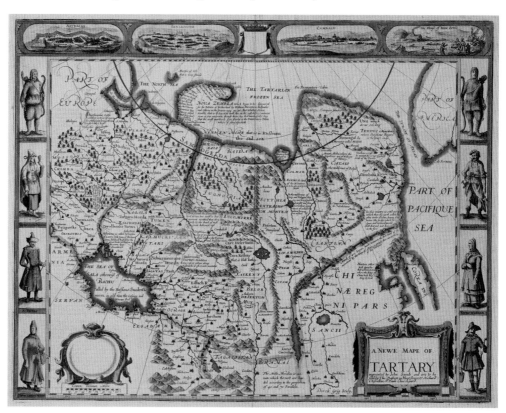

S/N **16982**

17th century English carte-à-figures map of Persia

28   SPEED, John.

The Kingdome of Persia with the cheef Citties and Habites described.

London: Thomas Bassett & Richard Chiswell, 1676. Coloured. 390 x 510mm.

A very decorative map of Persia, published in John Speed's 'Prospect of the Most Famous Parts of the World', the first English atlas of the world. It is decorated with four city prospects (Isfahan, Ormus, Tabriz & Gilan) along the top and with eight costume vignettes down the sides. The Caspian Sea still has not been mapped properly: it is shown wider than it is tall.

S/N **16745**

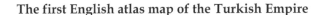

The first English atlas map of the Turkish Empire

29   SPEED, John.

The Turkish Empire.

London: Bassett & Chiswell, 1676. Coloured. 390 x 510mm. A few repairs, centre fold reinforced on verso.

Speed's map of the Turkish Empire, with ten costume vignettes down the sides and eight city prospects, including Constantinople, Jerusalem and Alexandria, along the top. On the verso a description of the Turkish Empire and the religious habits of its people. It was published in Speed's 'Prospect of the Most Famous Parts of the World', the first atlas of the world to be published in England, so illustrating the Ottoman Empire for the first time.

A classic collector's item.

TIBBETTS: 77.

S/N **17464**

Separately issued carte-à-figures map of Europe

30 DE WIT, Frederick.

Nova Europæ Descriptio.

Amsterdam, c.1660. Original colour. 445 x 555mm. Lower centrefold reinforced.

De Wit's first map of Europe, a carte-à-figures with six town prospects along the top and eight costumes of monarchs down the sides. The comparable map of Africa is dated 1660.

S/N **7679**

A rare English separate-issue map of Europe

31 OVERTON, John.

A New and most Exact map of Europe Described by NI Vischer and don into English and corected according to I. Bleau and Others with ye Habits of ye people & ye manner of ye cheife citties the like never before.

London, 1671. Coloured. 425 x 545mm. Trimmed to plate on all sides for binding, expertly re-margined with old paper, original binding folds flattened, tear from a fold repaired.

A very scarce panelled map of Europe, based on the Visscher issue of Keere's map of 1614, with borders decorated with costumes, town views and portraits of monarchs including Charles II. Originally issued in 1668, this is an example of the second state, with Overton's new address.

Apparently Overton was planning a world atlas and lacked maps of the continents, so had them engraved. As the matching map of Africa is signed by Philip Holmes the stylistic similarity makes it likely that Holmes also engraved the Europe. This world atlas never seems to have been published (although the British Library holds a bound collection of maps by Overton's son Henry containing this Europe); this example was issued as an illustration in a smaller-format book.

Little of Overton's output was original: he bought the stock of Peter Stent after his death from the plague in 1665, and c.1700 he bought the plates for Speed's county maps.

This is one of the scarcest 17th century maps of Europe published in England, rarely found undamaged.

S/N **15639**

An extremely rare map of Germany

32 BRUNN, Isaac.

Nova Germaniae Descriptio.

Strasbourg: Peter Aubrey, 1639. Two sheets conjoined, total 460 x 560mm. Minor repairs to folds.

A rare map of Germany, decorated with nine city prospects and two large panels of armorials of German cities. It was engraved by Isaac Brunn (1596 - post 1657).

First published in 1633, this second and final state has a dedication to Melchior de Insula instead of a prospect of Cologne.

Brunn's name is not in Tooley's Dictionary of Mapmakers.

S/N **15693**

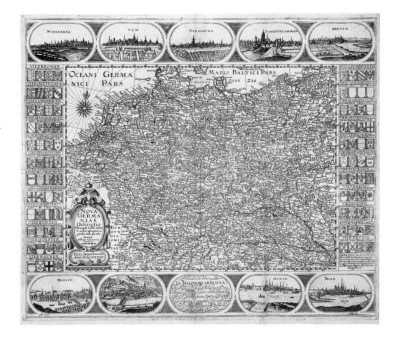

A scarce French carte-à-figures of Switzerland

33 BEREY, Nicolas.

Carte Generale des treze cantons de Suisse, Vallay ligues Grise, Maison-Dieu & Valteline. 1654.

Paris: Nicolas Langois, c.1675. Coloured. 405 x 520mm. Small repair at centre fold.

A rare map of Switzerland, a pirate copy of the map by Jodocus Hondius junior of 1630, itself a scarce map. The prospects along the top are Lucerne, St. Gallen, Bern, Solothurn and Schaffhausen, with larger views of Basel and Zurich in the bottom corners. The costume vignettes are pairs of nobles, merchants and peasants, men on the left and women on the right.

S/N **17721**

Classic carte-à-figures map of the Netherlands & Belgium

34 SPEED, John.

A New Mape of Ye XVII Provinces of Low Germanie, mended a new in manie places. Anno 1626.

London: George Humble, c.1627. Coloured. 410 x 525mm. Repairs to printed border at bottom.

The Netherlands, from Speed's 'Prospect of the... World', with ten costume vignettes down the sides and eight city prospects, including Antwerp, Amsterdam and Utrecht, along the top.

S/N **16112**

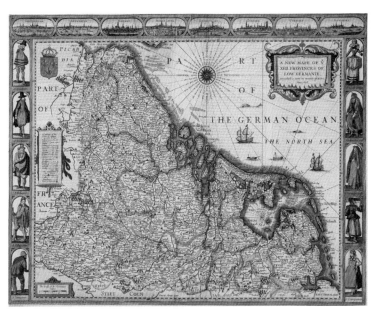

The first English atlas map of Denmark

35 SPEED, John.

The Kingdome of Denmarke...

London: George Humble, 1627. Old colour. 390 x 500mm. Re-margined at top.

Highly decorative map of Denmark, engraved by Evert Symonz van Hamersvelt for Speed's 'Prospect of the... World', with ten costume vignettes down the sides and six city prospects, including Copenhagen & Hamburg (as Holstein was still subject to Denmark at the time), along the top.

S/N **15642**

Carte-à-figures map of Bohemia

36 SPEED, John.

Bohemia.

London: Bassett & Chiswell, 1676. Coloured. 410 x 515mm. Re-margined at bottom, short repaired tear.

A fine map of Bohemia, from Speed's 'Prospect of the.. World'. At the top of this map are seven insets, showing views of Praguc, Comethau (Chomutov), Schlani (Slany), Lavn (Louny), Polm (Polna) and Czalsa, and of the 'Corte of the Emparer'. On the left and right sides are illustrations of Bohemians of five social ranks, from Queen to Countryman. Shown on the map are all the major settlements of Bohemia, and those belonging to neighbouring Germany, Moravia Silesia and Austria, stretching from Chemnitz to Silberberg (Zlotoryja) in the north, and from Munchen (Munich) to Wien (Vienna) in the south.

S/N **12287**

Classic English carte-à-figures map of Italy

37 SPEED, John.

Italia newly augmented by J: Speede.

London: Bassett & Chiswell, 1676. Coloured. 400 x 520mm. Small tear in margin repaired.

A superbly engraved map of Italy with eight vignettes of regional costume down the sides, as well as portraits of the Pope and the Doge of Venice, and views of Rome, Genoa, Verona, Naples, Venice and Florence running along the top.

From Speed's 'Prospect of the Most Famous Parts of the World', the first English atlas of the world.

S/N **17718**

JOHN SPEED'S 'THEATRE OF THE EMPIRE OF GREAT BRITAIN'

Speed's atlas of the British Isles was published before the birth of the carte-à-figures genre, but contained many of those features although in such a formalised layout. The maps, engraved by Jodocus Hondius in Amsterdam, feature town plans and views and arms of the local nobility and are favourites of the county map collectors.

The rare First Edition of Speed's map of the British Isles in contemporary colour

38 SPEED, John.

The Kingdome of Great Britaine and Ireland.

London: John Sudbury & George Humble, 1611-12. Contemporary colour. 385 x 510mm. Minor repairs to weaknesses caused by the original colour.

Speed has compiled the map from various sources: Saxton for England & Wales, Hondius's map of 1591 for Ireland & Mercator for Scotland. The two views show London c.1600, with St Pauls and the Tower on the north bank and the Globe and the Bear-baiting ring on the South; and Edinburgh, showing the city under siege c.1544.

Contemporary colour on Speed's maps is very unusual.

SHIRLEY: 316, catchword 'wee'.

S/N **17281**

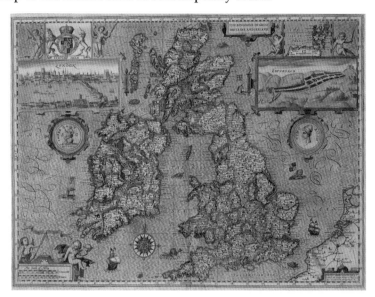

Speed's map of the Invasions of England

39 SPEED, John.

The Invasions of England & Ireland with al their Civill Wars Since the Conquest.

London: Thomas Bassett & Richard Chiswell, 1676. Coloured. 385 x 510mm.

A fascinating map of England, Wales and Ireland, showing the sites of battles 1066 - 1588, each with a little vignette scene. Of particular interest is the route of the Spanish Armada of 1588, from their entrance into the Channel, their crescent formation, their dispersal by the fireships and the trail of wrecks around the northern coasts. On the reverse is a companion text.

First issued in 1627, this map was engraved by Cornelius Danckerts from a prototype published by Speed c.1601 (of which Shirley notes only three known copies). It retains an obsolete form of the Isle of Man discarded by Speed in his map of 1611. It also holds a unique position in Speed's atlases, only appearing in volumes with the 'Theatre' and 'Prospect' combined: bound between the two were this map and four pages of accompanying text.

SHIRLEY: 397 (see 239 for the prototype).

S/N **17066**

The first British atlas map of Wales

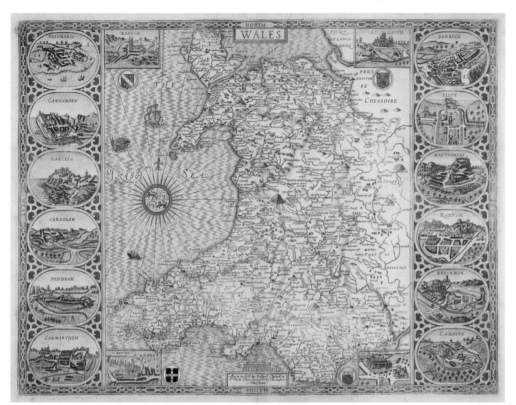

40   SPEED, John.

Wales.

London: Bassett & Chiswell, 1676. Coloured. 385 x 515mm. Repaired tear in bottom margin.

This is the most decorative map of Wales, with twelve large prospects of the Shire Towns, four smaller ones of the Cathedral Cities, four armorials and a large compass rose. As neither Saxton's atlas nor Camden's 'Britannia' contained a map of the country this is the first map of Wales to appear in a British atlas.

S/N **11544**

A map of Scotland with portraits of the Royal Family

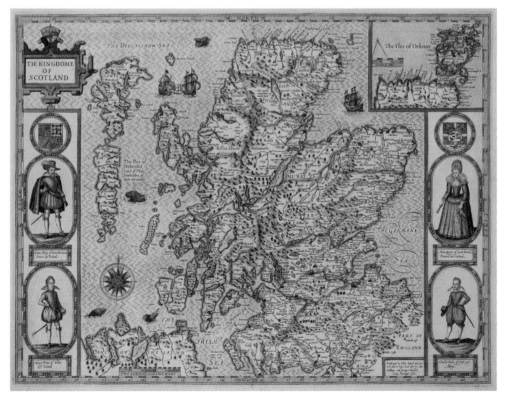

41   SPEED, John.

The Kingdome of Scotland.

London: John Sudbury & George Humble, 1616. Coloured. 390 x 510mm. A few marginal repairs; a very fine impression.

A rightly-famous map of Scotland, with an inset of the Orkneys. First issued 1611-12, this example comes from the second edition, planned for 1614 but delayed by the death of the printer William Hall. The vignette portraits are James VI of Scotland (also James I of England), his wife Anne and their two sons, Henry Prince of Wales & Charles (later Charles I).

In 1652 the Puritan ascendancy made it politic to re-engrave the plate: away went the Royal family, to be replaced by costume vignettes of a 'Scotch' (i.e. lowland) man & woman and their wilder 'Highland' neighbours.

S/N **17466**

An early edition of Speed's map of Cambridgeshire

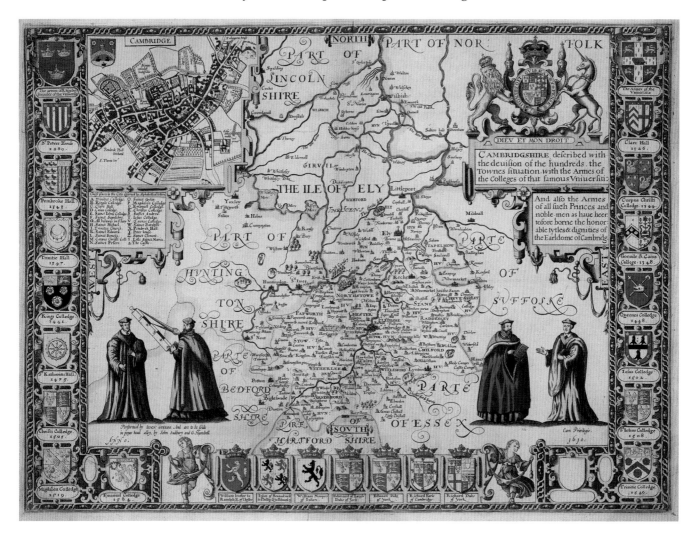

42 SPEED, John.

Cambridgshire described with the division of the hundreds, the townes situation with the Armes of the Colleges of that famous Universiti.

London: Sudbury & Humble, 1614-16. Coloured. 380 x 520mm, on thick paper. Minor repair in bottom margin.

Engraved by Jodocus Hondius, this is one of the most decorative maps of the county, with two columns of college arms, a plan of the city of Cambridge and the figures of four scholars.

This example was published in the second edition of John Speed's county atlas, the 'Theatre of the Empire of Great Britain', with an English-text history of the county on the reverse. The edition was planned for 1614 (the date on the titlepage of the English section), but the death of the printer William Hall delayed the publication until 1616.

S/N **17411**

Speed's famous map of Middlesex

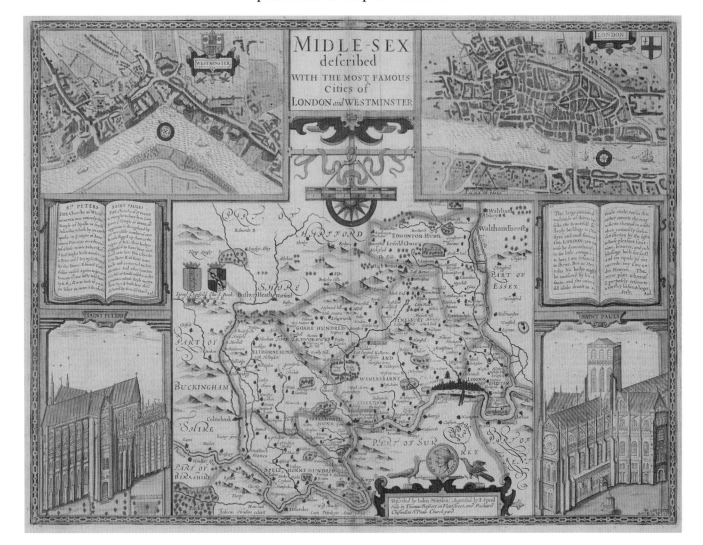

43   SPEED, John.

Midlesex described with the Most Famous Cities of London and Westminster. Described by John Norden...

London: Bassett & Chiswell, 1676. Coloured. 390 x 515mm. Crack in margin on right side, reinforced with archivist's tissue.

Map of Middlesex by John Speed, derived from the unpublished map by John Norden. Norden was a contemporary of Saxton and was the first to plan a series of county histories; however he failed to attract sufficient backing for his enterprise and never completed it. His surveying was superior to Saxton's, and Speed preferred to use Norden as a source where possible.

Engraved by Jodocus Hondius in 1610, the map has inset town plans of London and Westminster (also after Norden's surveys published 1593), and views of St Paul's and Westminster Cathedral.

SKELTON: 92.

S/N **12840**

John Speed's superb 17th century map of Cheshire

44   SPEED, John.

The Countye Palatine of Chester with that most ancient Citie described.

London: William Humble, 1646. 380 x 505mm. Minor restoration.

This map of Cheshire, engraved by Jodocus Hondius, is one of the most decorative maps of the county: two royal crests held aloft by putti, armorials, a plan of Chester and galleons and sea-monsters around the Wirall. The Latin text on verso gives a history of the county and an extensive list of towns and villages. Most of the Speed counties are derived from Saxton's maps: here Speed has used William Smith's revisions of Saxton, and the Braun & Hogenberg plan of Chester.

S/N **11632**

Speed's famous map of Surrey

45   SPEED, John.

Surrey Described and Divided into Hundreds.

London: William Humble, 1646. Coloured. 385 x 510mm. Unprinted top left corner border filled with mss.

One of the most decorative early maps of Surrey, engraved by Jodocus Hondius in 1610. Inset elevations of Richmond and Nonsuch Palaces, armorials, a compass rose and strapwork decorations add to its attractiveness.

By the time this edition was published the copper printing plate had been damaged, with the top left corner broken off.

S/N **16592**

THE SAXON HEPTARCHY

John Speed's map of Britain during the age of the Anglo-Saxon kingdoms is the classic decorative map of the British Isles. It shows England divided into the seven separate kingdoms (Northumbria, Mercia, East Anglia, Wessex, Essex, Sussex & Kent), with the kingdoms of the Scots, Picts and Welsh also marked. Flanking the map are two columns of vignettes: on the left are portraits of the first king of each realm; on the right are illustrations of the conversions of their successors to Christianity, persuaded by discussion, preaching, visions and violence.

Speed's map was so striking that it was copied by both Blaeu and Jansson for their atlases of the British Isles. Blaeu's version, published three decades after Speed's original, shows how map engraving had progressed: gone are the hatchured seas preferred by Jodocus Hondius, another Dutchman; the border decoration is more elaborate; and the engraving is more precise, making the map look much 'newer' than Speed's.

46 SPEED, John.

Britain As It Was Devided in the tyme of the Englishe Saxons especially during their Heptarchy.

London: William Humble, 1646. Coloured. 385 x 505mm. Minor repairs to margins.

The most decorative 17th century map of the British Isles, engraved by Jodocus Hondius for Speed's 'Theatre of the Empire of Great Britain'. First published in 1611, this comes from the 1646 edition, with the misprint 'Heptarcie' in the letterpress title on the reverse.

SHIRLEY: 587.

S/N **17697**

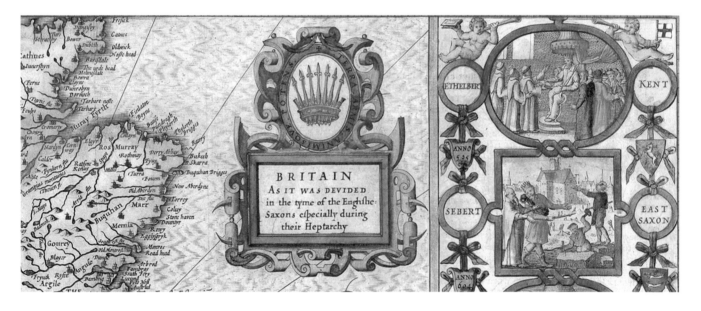

47 BLAEU, Johannes.

Britannia prout divisa fuit temporibus Anglo-Saxonium presertim durante illorum Heptarchia.

Amsterdam, 1642, Spanish text edition. Fine original colour. 415 x 530mm.

KOEMAN: Bl 66A.

S/N **17584**

Item 46

SEA CHARTS

Unlike the utilitarian Admiralty 'blue-back' charts of the 19th century, early sea charts were among the most beautiful printed maps: merchants whose vast wealth depended on ships sailing to the Indies were the purchasers of the sea atlases rather than navigators who would depend on written sailing guides and highly secret manuscript charts. Such atlases would be confined to libraries, where the galleons, sea monsters and compass roses that filled the oceans entertained the reader while he waited for his ships to return.

Breaking the Portuguese Monopoly on the East Indies Trade Routes

Sea charts from Linschoten's Itinerario

48   LINSCHOTEN, Jan Huygen van.

Typus orarum maritimarum Guineæ, Manicongo, & Angolæ ultra promontorium Bonæ Spei Usq... [&] Delineatio Orarum maritimarum, Terræ vulgo indigetatæ Terra do Natal...

Amsterdam, c.1596. Coloured. Two maps, c. 400 x 540mm. Backed with restorer's tissue.

Two highly decorative maps, engraved by Arnold van Langren for Linschoten's 'Itinerario', a sailing guide to the East Indies that broke the Portuguese monopoly on the trade routes. The western map shows the South Atlantic from Sierra Leone to the Cape of Good Hope, with inset coastal profiles of St Helena and Ascension Island, with a note describing the sirens swimming in Lake Zaire. The second shows the south east coast of Africa with Madagascar, to the Maldives and tips of India and Sri Lanka. Both are filled with decoration: ornate strapwork title and scale cartouches; compass roses, galleons and sea-monsters.

S/N **17222**

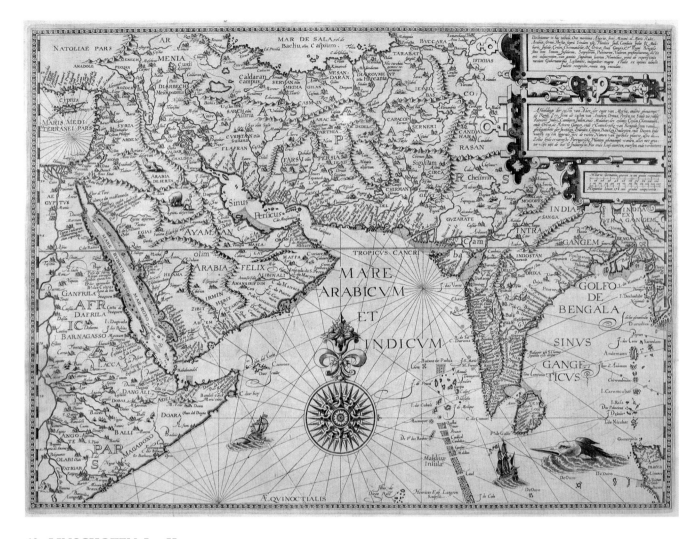

49 LINSCHOTEN, Jan Huygen van.

Deliniantur in hac tabula, Orae maritimae Abexiae freti Mecani: al. Maris Rubri: Arabiae, Ormi, Persiae...

Amsterdam, c.1596. 390 x 540mm, with unusually generous margins.

Engraved by Henricus van Langren, this chart displays all the features that made this period the golden age of decorative cartography: the titles, in Latin and Dutch, are within a strapwork cartouche, also including the scales; across the Indian Ocean is a large, finely-engraved compass rose, surmounted by a fruit garland; sea-monsters and galleons fill the seas, while a lion, elephant and camel appear in Arabia, and just south of Delhi are a pair of unicorns.

The map shows Cyprus top left, Bokhara and Samarkand top right, Sumatra bottom right and Ethiopia bottom left, with Delhi, Bahrain and Kabul named. All are synonymous with the famed riches of the East, the inspiration for the Itinerario.

TIBBETS: 46.

S/N **17696**

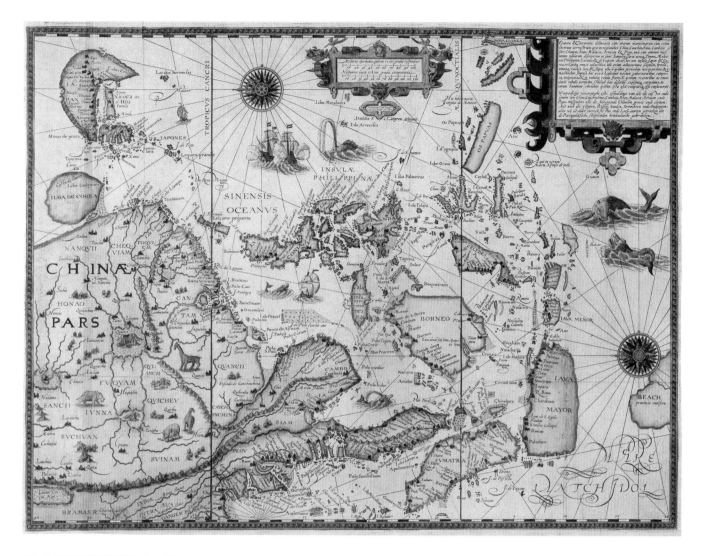

50   LINSCHOTEN, Jan Huygen van.

Exacta et accurata delineatio cum orarum maritimarum...

Amsterdam, c.1596. Coloured. Two sheets conjoined as issued, total 395 x 530mm. Restoration at bottom margin.

This chart of the Far East, orientated with north to the left, was engraved by Henricus van Langren after Arnold Florent van Langren. It shows Burma, Sumatra and the Malay Peninsula, Borneo and the Philippines, around the coast of China to Korea & Japan. Korea is an almost round island; Japan is described by Walter as 'shrimp-shaped'.

On the right edge is 'Beach, the Gold Province', often taken for Australia. This derives from Marco Polo's 'Locach', a place the Chinese told him was far to the south. In a 1552 edition of Grynaeus's 'Novus Orbis Regionum' the name was mis-transcribed to 'Boeach', then shortened to Beach. However today it is believed that 'Lochach' was 'Lo-huk', the Cantonese name for Lopburi, a kingdom in southern Thailand.

Among the vignettes filling the gaps in China are an elephant, camel, giraffe and rhinoceros.

WALTER 12.

S/N **16966**

Dudley's rare sea chart of Iceland, with the mythical island of Frisland

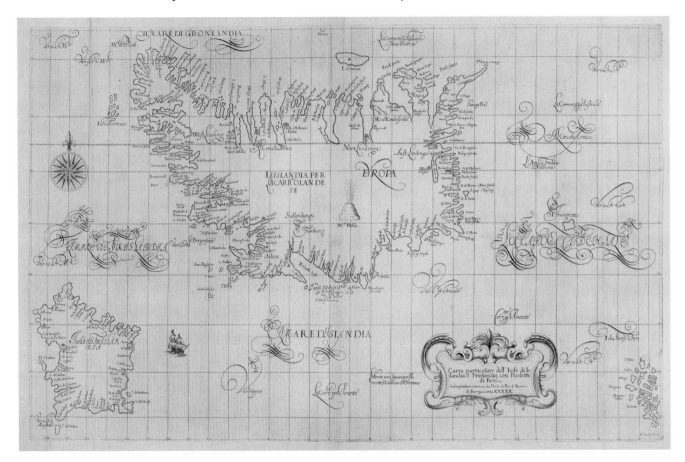

51   DUDLEY, Robert.

Carta particolare dell'Isole di Islandia è Frislandia, con l'Isolette di Faré. La longitudine cimincia da l'Isla di Pico d'Arores. di Europa Carta XXXXX.

Florence: Francesco Onofri, 1646-7. 485 x 760mm.

A spectacular sea-chart of Iceland, engraved in Antonio Francesco Lucini's unique style for Dudley's 'Dell'Arcano del Mare' (Secrets of the Sea), an encyclopaedia of maritime knowledge. All the detail of Iceland is coastal apart from the vignette of the volcano Hekla erupting. To the south west is what must be the largest depiction of the mythical island of Frisland (16cm north to south), with over 50 names!

The 'Arcano' was the first sea-atlas by an Englishman to be printed (albeit engraved and published in Italy), breaking the Dutch monopoly of such publications. The engraver Lucini wrote in the introduction to the second edition that he worked for 12 years on the copper plates, which weighed 5000 lbs. It is Lucini's florid style of lettering that makes the chart stand out: the italic scrip is as eye-catching as the title cartouche, galleon or compass rose.

Dudley was the son of the Earl of Leicester, favourite of Queen Elizabeth I, and was born in secret to avoid her jealousy. Well educated, he joined the Elizabethan maritime adventurers and led an expedition to the Orinoco in 1594, raiding Trinidad en route. After failing to prove his parents married, which would allow him to assume his father's titles, he left England for Italy in 1605. There he assumed the titles of 'Earl of Warwick and Leicester' and 'Duke of Northumberland' in 1620, which caused James I to seize all Dudley's English properties. He died in 1649, two years after the first edition of the 'Arcano'.

S/N **17271**

Rare edition of Doncker's chart of the Mediterranean

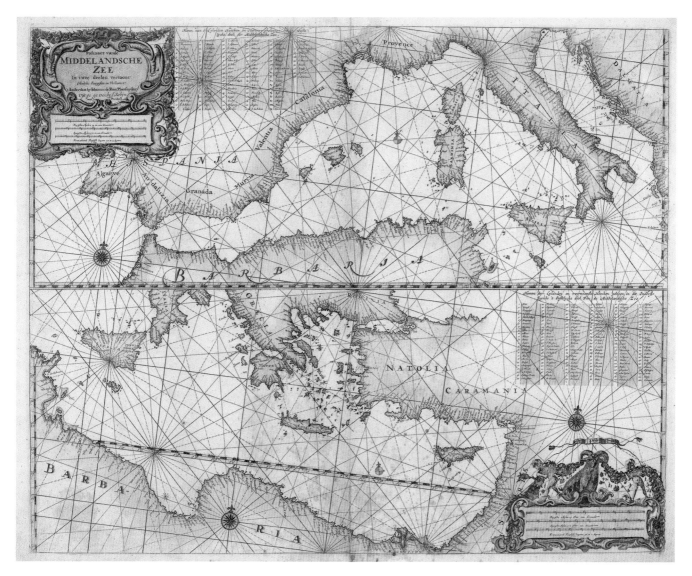

52   DONCKER, Hendrik.

Paskaart van de Middelandsche Zee in twee deelen vertoont.

Amsterdam: Johannes de Ram & Jacobus Robijn, c.1683. Old colour. 515 x 590mm. Minor reinforcing at centre fold.

An extremely rare edition of Doncker's chart of the Mediterranean in two sections, first published 1660. It has been updated with more ornate cartouches for title and scale, the latter depicting a ram with a star on its forehead, a pun on the publisher's name which works in English as well as Dutch.

Johannes de Ram (1648-93), formerly a timber merchant, set himself up as a map publisher by buying old printing plates. This chart was published in association with Jacobus Robijn (1649-c.1710), although there is no mention of this partnership in Koeman's 'Atlantes Neerlandici'.

S/N **17601**

A superb chart of the Far East and Australia

53   DE WIT, Frederick.

Orientaliora Indiarum Orientalium cum Insulis Adjacentibus à Promontorio C.Comorin ad Japan. Pascaaert van t'Oosert gedeelte van Oost Indien van C. Comorin tot Iapan

Amsterdam, c.1688. Fine colour, with gold highlights. 445 x 545mm. A very fine impression on heavy paper, bottom centre fold strengthened on verso.

De Wit's famous chart of the East Indies and Australia, orientated with north to the left. Japan appears top left and Australia, according to Tasman, top right.

Published in the 'Orbis Maritimus ofte Zee Atlas', with a fine title cartouche representing the wealth possible from the East India trade in full colour.

TOOLEY: Australia, p.1369, plate 100; WALTER: 40, illus; KOEMAN: Wit 16.

S/N **16648**

A 17th century sea chart of the north Pacific and Siberia

54   GOOS, Pieter.

Noordoost Cust van Asia van Japan tot Nova Zembla.

Amsterdam, c.1680. Old colour. 450 x 550mm. A few signs of age.

A scarce Dutch sea chart showing the coast of mainland Asia from the Bohai Sea in China north and west around Siberia to Novaya Zemlya, with Korea correctly shown as a peninsula, Japan and the partial outlines of Eso and 'Compagnies Land'. The title is on a blanket over the back of a camel, with a rider and two walkers.

S/N **17602**

A pair of 17th century sea charts of the Indian Ocean with Australia

55   GOOS, Pieter.

Paskaerte zynde t'Oosterdeel Van Oost Indien, met alle de Eylanden daer ontrendt gelegen van C. Comorin tot aen Japan.[&] Pascaerte Van't Westelycke Deel van Oost Indien, Van Capo de Bona Esperanca tot C. Comerin.

Amsterdam, c.1680. Old colour. Each c. 445 x 545mm. A few signs of age. Far East with small tear in lower centrefold restored, entering the printed surface by 2cm; small area of verdigris weakness reinforced with archivist's tape, hardly noticeable from the front.

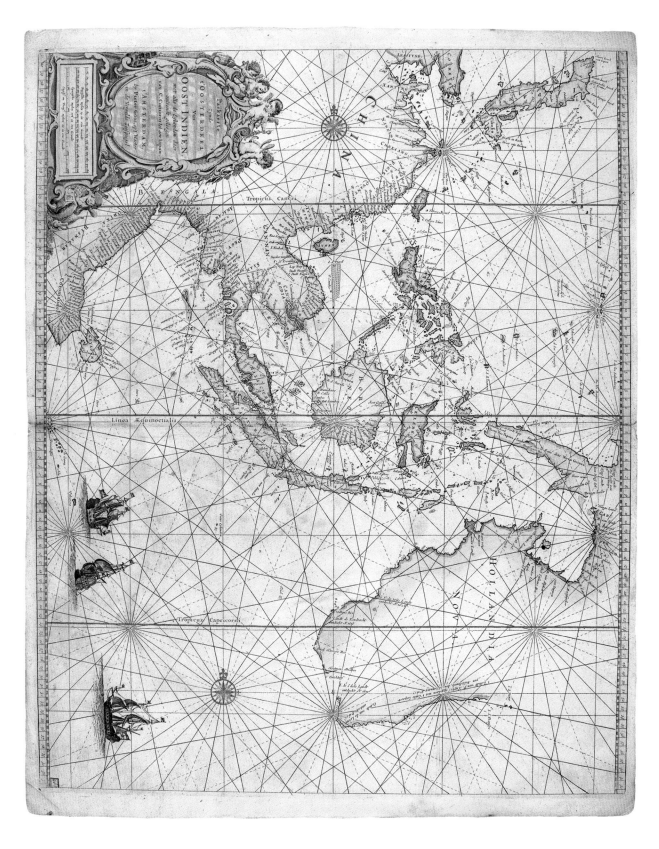

A pair of decorative sea charts showing from from the Cape of Good Hope to northern and western Australia, orientated with north to the left, including Sri Lanka, Japan and the Philippines and the western coasts of New Guinea and Australia.

The Dutch discoveries in northern Australia are marked, including those of Abel Tasman's second voyage of 1644, although Tasmania, discovered by him in 1642, is omitted.

S/N **17621**

**The most famous chart of the
Mediterranean Sea**

56 HOOGHE, Romeyn de.

Carte Nouvelle de la Mer Mediterranee ou
sont Exactement Remarques Tous les Ports,
Golfes, Rochers, Bancs de Sable &c.

*Amsterdam: Pierre Mortier, 1694. Original
colour refreshed. Three sheets conjoined, total
585 x 1390mm. Minor repairs.*

A monumental chart of the Mediterranean
Sea, with 38 insets of harbours, all in full
colour. Throughout the seas are numerous
galleons and galleys, while allegorical
figures and sea monsters adorn the insets.

The chart appeared in one part of
Mortier's 'Neptune François', titled 'Cartes
Marines a l'Usage des Armées du Roy de
la Grande Bretagne'. The nine charts of this
section, all engraved by Romeyn de
Hooghe, one of the foremost artist/etchers
of the period, was described by Koeman as
the 'most spectacular type of maritime
cartography ever produced in 17th century
Amsterdam'; the Mediterranean is the
largest and most intricately decorated of
the nine.

Mortier's motives in the production of this
atlas was to flatter the Dutch king on the
British throne since the Glorious
Revolution of 1688, William III, to whom it
is dedicated. The unprecedented size of the atlas and the use of artists such as de Hooghe were not cheap: Koeman
calls it the 'most expensive sea atlas' of the period, 'intended more as a show-piece than something to be used by
the pilots at sea'.

KOEMAN: M. Mor 5, and vol iv p.424.

S/N **14471**

Monumental sea chart of south-east England

57 HOOGHE, Romeyn de.

Carte Nouvelle des Costes d'Angleterre depuis la Riviere de la Tamise jusques à Portland.

*Amsterdam: Pierre Mortier, 1693. Coloured. Two sheets conjoined, total 600 x 950mm. Some restoration, laid on archival
paper.*

A superb chart of south-east England showing the Thames to London, and the sea coast round to Portland with the
Isle of Wight and Alderney, an inset detail of the Strait of Dover and prospects of Portsmouth and Rochester &
Chatham.

KOEMAN: vol 4. p. 423-4, M.Mor 5.

S/N **16922**

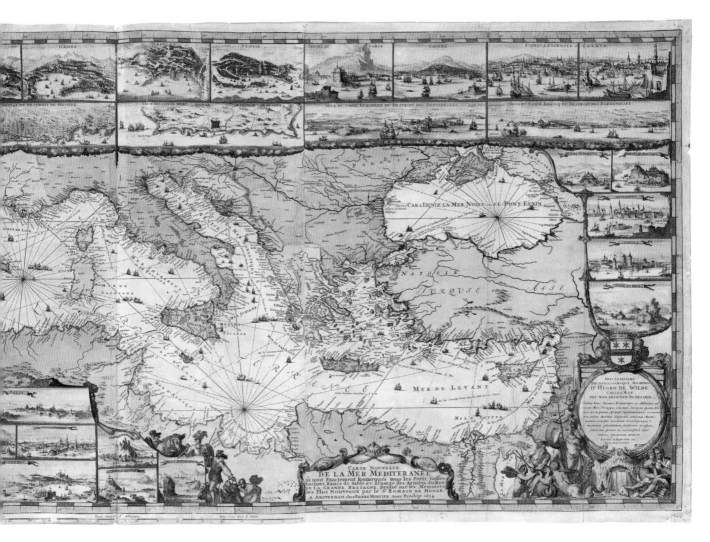

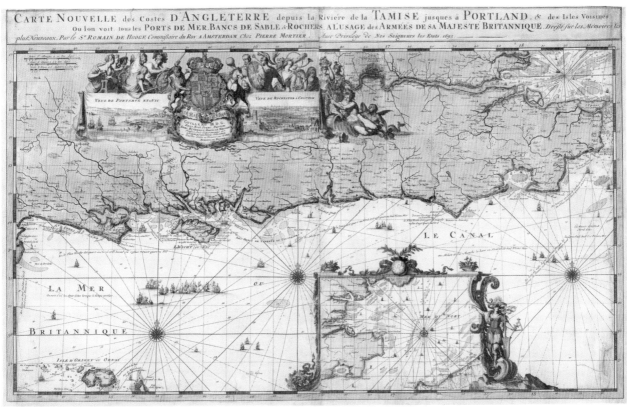

Item 57

THE IMAGINATION OF HEINRICH BÜNTING

Bünting's 'Itinerarium Sacrae Scripturae' was an odd concept: a rewriting of the Bible as a travel book. Considering that Heinrich Bünting (1545-1606) was a Protestant pastor his choice of inspiration for the maps is even more bizarre. However the eccentricity made the book popular, with editions issued for over fifty years

Bünting's commentary on the Bible with his famous figurative maps

58   BÜNTING, Heinrich.

Itinerarium Sacrae Scripturae, Das ist: Ein Reisebuch uber die gantze heilige Schrifft.

Magdeburg: Paul Donat for Ambrosius Kirchners,1595, German edition. Folio, Title-page to part one printed in red and black, title-page to part II with woodcut battle scene. Contemporary blind-tooled panelled pigskin over bevelled boards, with two brass clasps; four parts in one; 9 double-page maps, 2 single page, 1 double-page plate. One map and one plate with minor repairs to edges.

A fine example of Bünting's most famous book, containing three of the most famous cartographical curiosities: the 'clover-leaf' world map, with Jerusalem at the centre; Europe depicted as a queen; and Asia depicted as Pegasus, the winged horse. Also there are more conventional maps of Africa and the Old World (although the silhouette of the European Queen can still be discerned) and other maps of the Holy Land and Egypt.

SHIRLEY: World 142 & 143; NORWICH: Africa 17; MCC 1: Geographical Oddities 2 & 3.

S/N **16606**

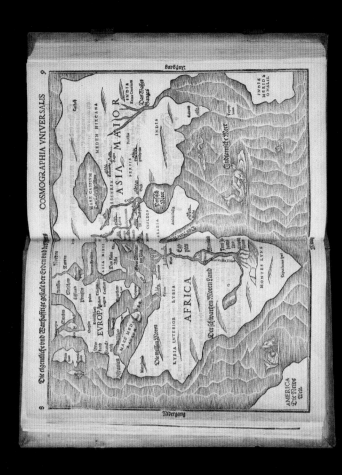

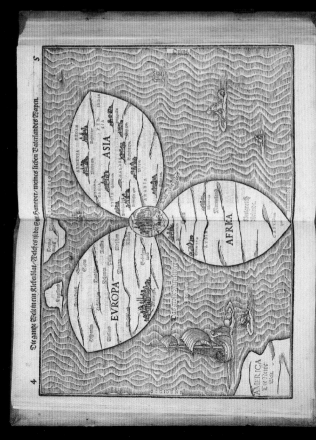

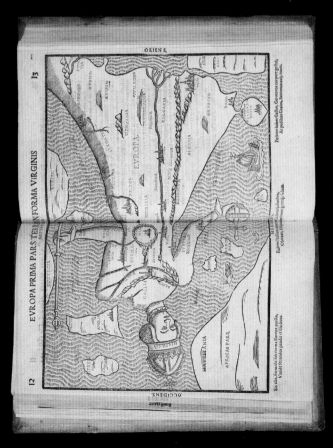

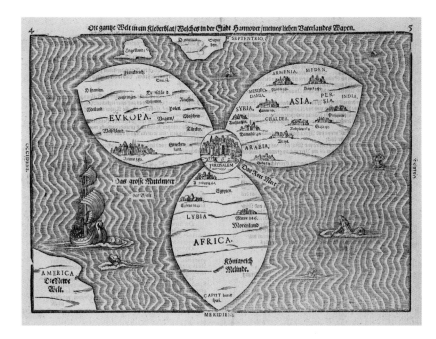

**Bünting's famous clover leaf map
of the world**

59 BÜNTING, Heinrich.

Die ganze Welt in ein Kleberblat...

*Magdeburg, 1581-. Woodcut, printed area
270 x 380mm. A fine, dark printing.*

Bünting's famous clover leaf map,
showing Europe, Asia and Africa as
separate leaves connected to Jerusalem
at the centre. England and Scandinavia
appear as islands at the top of the map;
the New World fills the bottom left
corner.

The map was published in Bünting's
'Itinerarium Sacræ Scripturæ' (Travel
through Holy Scripture), a reworking of
the bible as a travel guide. Also
included were maps of Europe as a
Virgin Queen and Asia as Pegasus.

This design was of particular relevance
to Bünting because a clover leaf features
on the arms of his hometown of
Hanover.

SHIRLEY: World 142.

S/N **17369**

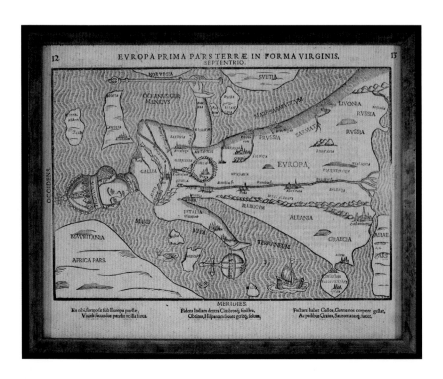

Fantasy map of Europe as a Queen

60 BÜNTING, Heinrich.

Europa Prima Pars Terræ in Forma
Virginis.

*Magdeburg, 1581-, German edition.
Woodcut, printed area 300 x 370mm. Some
old ink marginalia.*

The famous fantasy map depicting
Europe as a Virgin Queen, with Iberia
her head and crown; Denmark her right
arm; Italy her left arm with Sicily an orb
in her hand; Greece, the Balkans and
Russia her skirts; and Bohemia a
medallion on a chain over her heart.

S/N **16838**

A copper-engraved version of Europe as a Virgin Queen

61 BÜNTING, Heinrich.

Europa Prima Pars Terræ in Forma Virginis.

Brunswick: Emmeran Kirchnern, 1646, German text edition. 260 x 360mm. Trimmed to plate at sides, as issued.

A copper-engraved version of Europe as a Virgin Queen, with crown, orb and sceptre. Iberia forms her head and crown; Denmark her right arm; Italy her left arm with Sicily an orb in her hand; Greece, the Balkans and Russia her skirts; and Bohemia a medallion on a chain around her neck.

Although the title and text under the map are in Latin, the text on verso is German.

S/N **17586**

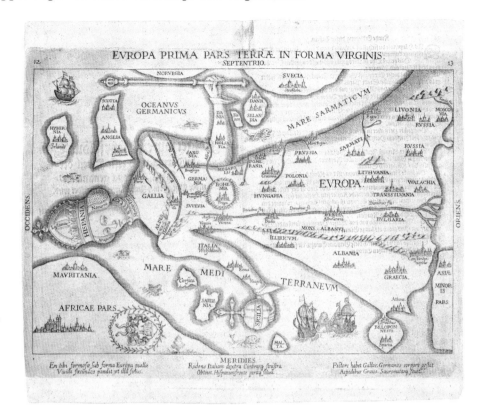

A copper-engraved version of Asia as Pegasus

62 BÜNTING, Heinrich.

Asia Secunda pars Terræ in Forma Pegasi.

Brunswick: Emmeran Kirchnern, 1646, German text edition. 260 x 360mm. Narrow lateral margins.

A copper-engraved version of Asia as Pegasus, the winged horse, originally published as a woodcut. The head is Turkey and Armenia, the wings Scythia and Tartary, forelegs Arabia, hind legs India and the Malay Peninsula.

Although the title and text under the map are in Latin, the text on verso is German.

S/N **17585**

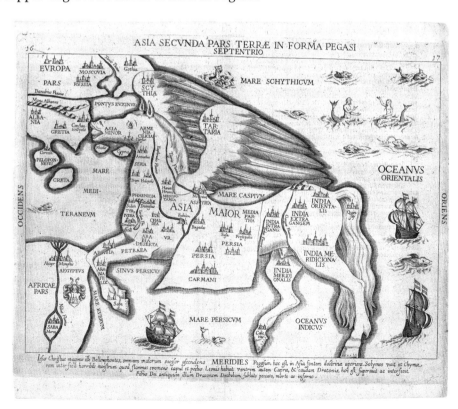

CREATURES

Bünting was not the first mapmaker to include fantastical creatures; nor was he the last. Below are a selection of maps that owe more to the imagination than reality.

One of the earliest world maps available to the collector, decorated with bizarre creatures

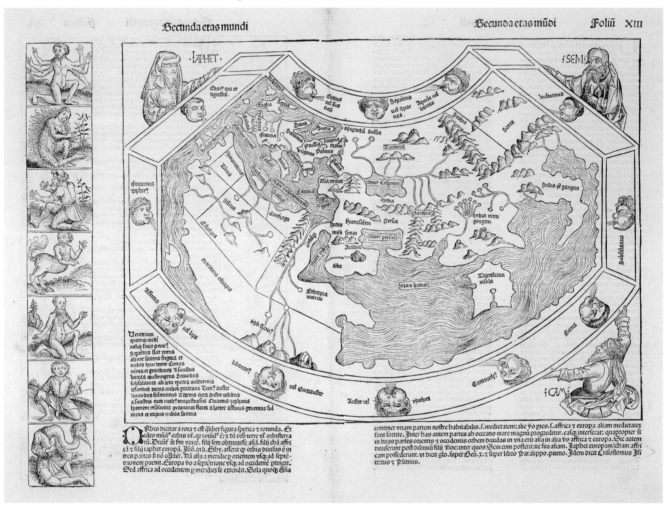

63   SCHEDEL, D. Hartmann.

[World.]

Nuremberg: Anton Koberger, 1493, Latin text edition. Woodcut, printed area 370 x 520mm, good margins.

A fine example of the famous incunable world map from the 'Nuremberg Chronicle', published a matter of months after Columbus' return to Spain after his first voyage to the New World, so including nothing of his discoveries. Instead, appropriately for a history of the world, it takes a retrospective view, with the cartography that of Ptolemy, with a land-locked Indian Ocean with the island of Taprobana, but given a biblical theme by depicting the three sons of Noah in the borders. Down the left are seven vignettes of mythological creatures, with a further 14 on the reverse, taken from the works of Herodotus, Solinus and Pliny. These include figures with six arms, four eyes or a bird-neck and a centaur. The text describes which parts of the world they inhabit.

SHIRLEY: 19.

S/N **17465**

The famous map of Iceland with sea monsters, in superb original colour

64 ORTELIUS, Abraham.

Islandia.

Antwerp, 1598, French text edition. Fine original colour. 390 x 490mm. Old ink mss. changing pagination from 103 to 104 (both numbers used in this edition according to van den Broecke).

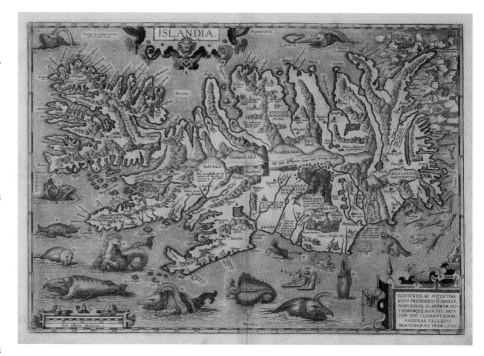

One of the most decorative maps ever published, well-known for its depiction of over a dozen exotic sea-monsters (with a key referring to a list on verso), polar bears on iceflows and the volcano Hekla in the interior.

Ortelius based the cartography on a map by Gudbrandur Thorlaksson (1542-1627), Lutheran bishop of Hólar, which was the most accurate up to that time. However he augmented the map with the sea monsters from the woodcut 'Carta Marina' of Scandinavia by Olaus Magnus, 1539.

Ortelius's version first appeared in an atlas in the 'Additamentum IV', an appendix of new 22 maps not featured in the last full 'Theatrum Orbis Terrarum', 1587. This example was printed eight years later.

VAN DEN BROECKE: 161.

S/N **17303**

Munster's famous woodblock illustrating Sea Monsters

65 MUNSTER, Sebastian.

De regnis septentrion. Monstra marina & terrestria, quæ passim in partibus aquilonis inueniuntur.

Basle, c.1560, Latin text edition. Coloured woodcut, printed area 280 x 350mm.

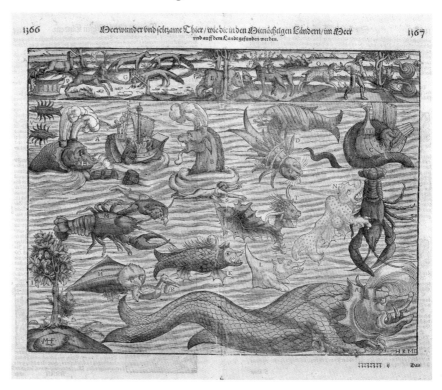

Munster's famous woodcut of sea monsters, based on Olaus Magnus' 'Carta Marina' of 1539. Besides a lobster large enough to hold an unfortunate sailor in its claw, there are monsters with the heads of a dog, boar, owl & bull: tusks, horns and twin-spouts abound. One vignette shows a galleon trying to outrun one monster by throwing their cargo overboard. Many of these monsters were adapted by Ortelius for his map of Iceland in 1587.

S/N **17694**

The famous 'Leo Belgicus' map

66   STRADA, Famiano.

De Bello Belgico Decas Prima. Famiani Stradæ Rom. Soc. Iesu.

Rome, c.1632. 320 x 220mm. Old ink mss. in margins.

The famous map of the Netherlands depicted as a 'Leo Belgicus'. The lion faces right, with the title on a shield held upright by the lion's right paw. It appeared as the engraved titlepage of the Jesuit Strada's history of the Belgian wars, first published 1632.

MCC 7: Tooley, Leo Belgicus 15, plate VII.

S/N **17699**

Johann Bayer's Constellations

A selection of creatures engraved by Alexander Mair for Bayer's 'Uranometria', a star atlas that shaped the way the heavens would be perceived for more than two centuries.

Ulm: Johann Gorlini, 1639. Coloured, with gold highlights. 285 x 380mm.

67 [Hydra.]

S/N **14613**

68 [Cetus.]

S/N **14610**

69 [Delphinus.]

S/N **14593**

70 [Piscis Notius.]

S/N **14580**

71 [Ursa Minor.]

S/N **14602**

72 [Ophiuchus Serpentarius.]

S/N **14584**

73 [Draco.]

S/N **14587**

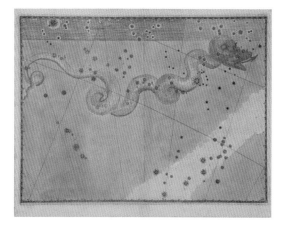

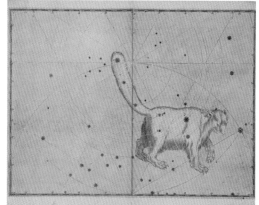

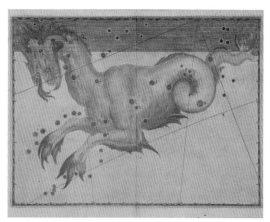

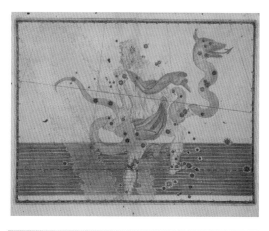

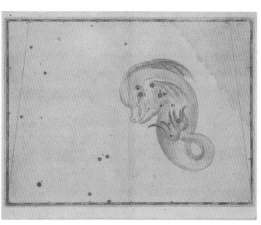

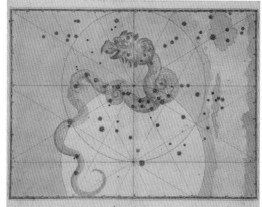

TEL: +44 (0)20 7491 0010

CARICATURE

Maps have also been popular for caricature, allowing the artist to illustrate national stereotypes - and vendettas!

Dighton's famous caricature maps of England and Scotland

Item 74   Item 75

74 DIGHTON, Robert.

Caricature of England and Wales.

London: Bowles & Carver, c.1808. Original colour. Card, 140 x 105mm.

A separate-issue card, reduced from Dighton's famous 'Geography Bewitched' caricature map. England is a pot-bellied man, foaming mug of beer in his hand, pipe in his mouth, sitting astride a scaly sea-monster. Wales is his jacket.

Outside the printed border a text 'Caricatures of Ireland, Scotland, &c. with other ingenious devices' advertises the other maps in the series.

S/N **17716**

75 DIGHTON, Robert.

A Caricature Scotland. Geography bewitched. Bonny Scotia.

London: Bowles & Carver, c.1808. Original colour. Card, 140 x 105mm.

A separate-issue card, reduced from Dighton's famous 'Geography Bewitched' caricature map. Scotland is depicted as an ugly man kneeling on a tasselled cushion, holding a tartan bag behind his back.

S/N **17717**

Caricature map of England, from Gillray's cruder output

76   GILLRAY, James.

A New Map of England & France. The French Invasion; or John Bull, bombarding the Bum-Boats.

London: Henry George Bohn, 1851. Coloured etching. 350 x 260mm.

A satirical map of England, shown divided into counties, with Durham sporting the face of George III with Northumberland his nightcap, East Anglia his knee, Kent his foot and Sussex his buttock. The king is voiding his bowels on the French bumboats (derived from the Dutch for a canoe, 'boomschuit', and meaning a small boat used to ferry supplies to ships moored offshore) trying to cross the Channel.

The caricature was drawn and etched by James Gillray (under the pseudonym 'John Schoebert') and originally published by Hannah Humphrey in 1793, at a time when England was in terror of an invasion by the French revolutionaries. In among the bombardment are the words 'British Declaration', referring to George's promise to return Toulon (held by Royalists aided by British and Spanish forces) to French on the restoration of the Bourbon monarchy.

This example, printed from the original plate, was published in Bohn's 'Historical and Descriptive Account of the Caricatures of James Gillray', the most complete edition of Gillray's work, including the coarser 'Suppressed Plates'.

British Museum Satires 8346.

S/N **16754**

Aleph's Pictorial Maps

A series of maps published in 'Geographical Fun', a charming atlas of caricature maps of European countries, drawn, according to the preface, by a fifteen-year-old girl to amuse her sick brother. The author was, however, William Harvey (1796-1873), a London Doctor and Journalist, best-known for his book 'London Scenes and London People', 1863. The maps contain many references to the political changes sweeping through continental Europe, with representations of Garibaldi and Bismarck.

London: Hodder & Stoughton, 1869. each map c.250 x 210mm.

77   England.

The text below the image reads, ''Beautiful England, - on her Island throne, - Grandly she rules, - with half the world her own; From her vast empire the sun ne'er departs: She reigns a Queen - Victoria, Queen of Hearts''.

S/N **17235**

78   Wales.

''Geography bewitch'd - Owen Glendowr, In Bardic grandeur, looks from shore to shore, And sings King Arthur's long, long pedigree, and cheese and leeks, and knights of high degree''.

S/N **17234**

79   Scotland.

''A gallant piper, struggling through the bogs, His wind bag broken, wearing his clay clogs; Yet strong of heart, a fitting emblem makes, For Scotland - land of heroes and of cakes''.

S/N **17270**

80   Ireland.

''And what shall typify the Emerald Isle? A Peasant, happy in her baby's smile? No fortune her's, though rich in native grace, - Herrings, potatoes, and a joyous face''.

S/N **17236**

81   Prussia.

"His Majesty of Prussia - grim and old - Sadowa's King - by needle guns made bold; With Bismarck of the royal conscience, keeper, In dreams political none wiser - deeper"

S/N **17244**

Other European countries are available on our web site

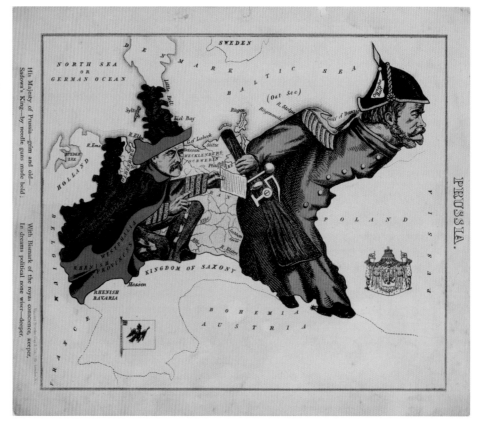

Item 81

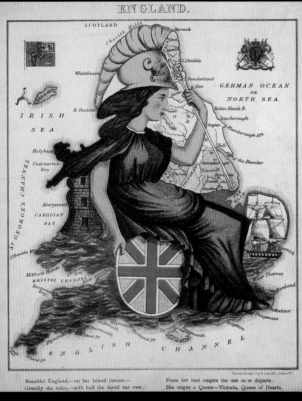

England.

Beautiful England,—on her Island throne,—
Grandly she rules,—with half the world her own;
From her vast empire the sun ne'er departs:
She reigns a Queen—Victoria, Queen of Hearts.

Item 77

Wales.

Geography bewitch'd—Owen Glendowr,
In Bardic grandeur, looks from shore to shore,
And sings King Arthur's long, long pedigree,
And cheese and leeks, and knights of high degree.

Item 78

Scotland.

A gallant piper, struggling through the bogs,
His wind bag broken, wearing his clay clogs;
Yet, strong of heart, a fitting emblem makes
For Scotland—land of heroes and of cakes.

Item 79

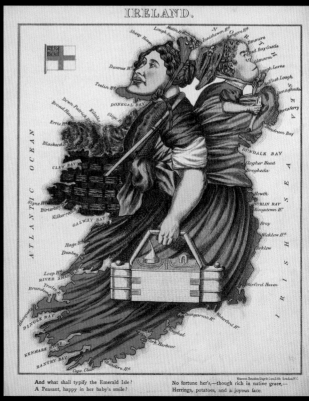

Ireland.

And what shall typify the Emerald Isle?
A Peasant, happy in her baby's smile?
No fortune her's,—though rich in native grace,—
Herrings, potatoes, and a joyous face.

Item 80

An Italian map satirising the British Empire as a serpent

82   GROSSI, Augusto.

Allegoria sull'Impero Inglese.

Bologna: Il Papagallo, 1878. Chromolithograph. Sheet 410 x 610mm.

An Italian satirical map showing the globe being turned by a devil of 'Progress' and an angel 'Civilization'. Wrapped around it is a snake with a lion's head, marked 'British Empire in India'. The head, resting on Ireland, has human figures in its mouth; the body crushes others in Gibraltar, Egypt, India, Australia, China, Canada, Cape Colony, Transvaal and Mauritius. Watching from the side lines are men wrapped in shrouds with garlands, including Victor Emmanuel II, politicians Adolphe Thiers & Giuseppe Mazzini and Italian poets Virgil, Dante and Tasso.

'Il Papagallo' was a satirical magazine founded in January 1873 by Augusto Grossi (1835-1919), which specialised in colour-printed caricatures like this one. At its peak circulation reached 50,000, and in 1878 a Parisian version, 'Le Perroquet', and London edition, 'The Parrot', were launched. 'Il Papagallo' closed in 1915, when Grossi was 70 years old.

This example is apparently unrecorded. Other examples we have traced have the title in the box lower right, with Grossi's name next to it. Here the title has been replaced by a French description, suggesting it was published in Bologna for the French magazine.

S/N **17537**

A famous English caricature map of Europe

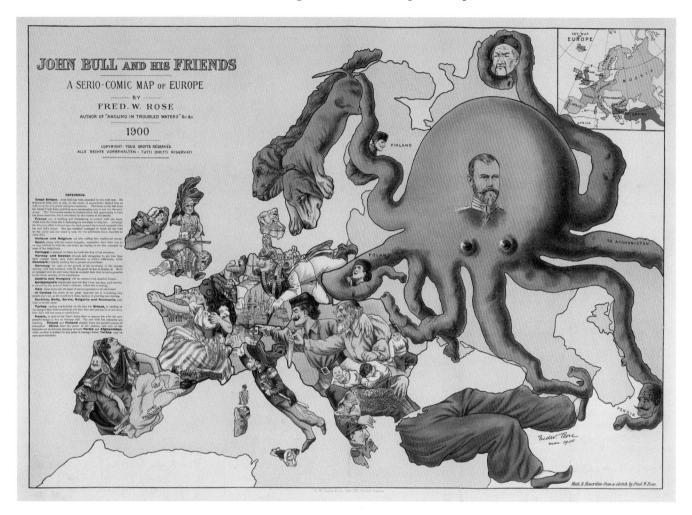

83   ROSE, Frederick W.

John Bull and his Friends. A Serio-Comic Map Of Europe by Fred. W. Rose, Author of 'Angling in Troubled Waters' &c &c. Matt. B. Hewerdine from a sketch by Fred. W. Rose.

London: G.W. Bacon & Co, 1900. Chromolithograph, printed area 490 x 685mm. Binding folds reinforced on verso, as usual with this map.

The famous map of Europe made up of caricatures of each country, highlighting the insecurities of the time, as explained by the text on the left. The main worry is the Russian octopus with the face of Tsar Nicolas II, with tentacles wrapped around the throats of Poland, Persia and China, one grabbing for Turkey's foot and another laid across Finland. England and Scotland are depicted as a soldier in tropical uniform, waving a Union Jack, with two wildcats, marked 'Orange Free State' and 'Transvaal', savaging his legs. He sits on shells marked with their destinations: India, Canada, South Africa and Australia. Ireland 'vents her abuse' on him. France beckons Germany to help her against Britain who she blames for her colonial upsets, and Italy stretches out a helping hand. Spain is mourning the recent loss of Cuba and the Philippines, her last important colonial possessions.

Rose (1849-1915) produced at least three maps of Europe in the same style, the first in 1877, one in 1899 and this the last, in which he was aided by book-illustrator Matthew Bede Hewerdine (1868-1909).

S/N **17293**

A Japanese variant of the serio-comic map

84 OHARA, Kisaburo.

[Japanese title.] A Humorous Diplomatic Atlas of Europe and Asia.

Tokyo: Yoshijiro Yabuzaki, 1904. Chromolithograph, sheet 495 x 560mm.

A variant of the Frederick W. Rose 'octopus' map of Europe, extended to include more Asian states, including India, Tibet, China, Korea and Japan, with a title in Japanese and English, an English description top left and a longer Japanese text under the map.

It was drawn by a student at Keio University on the outbreak of the Russo-Japanese War in 1904 so, of course, the focal point of the map is the 'Black Octopus' of Russia. One of its tentacles reaches down to Port Arthur in Manchuria, which was Japan's first target of the hostilities. Ohara gloatingly writes 'The Japanese fleet has already practically annihilated Russia's naval powers in the Orient. The Japanese army is about to win a signal victory over Russia in Corea and Manchuria'.

SOUCACOS: p.178.

S/N **17455**

A serio-comic map of Europe for the First World War

85 AMSCHEWITZ, John Henry.

European Revue. Kill That Eagle.

London: Geographia Ltd, 1914. Colour-printed wood engraving. Sheet 540 x 780mm. Repairs to binding folds, repaired tear left of title.

A serio-comic map of Europe on the outbreak of the Great War. John Bull, in Union Jack waistcoat and riding boots, strides across the English Channel, rolling up his sleeves, sword in hand. To his left are soldiers from Ireland, Canada, Australia and India. France is a figure of Marianne, sticking a bayonet into the eagle of Imperial Germany. The Russian bear is clawing at the ankle of the Austrian pierrot. Italy is a singer with a song sheet 'You Made Me Love You, I Didn't Want to Do It'. Scandinavia, Iberia and Switzerland are onlookers in various levels of distress.

John Henry Amschewitz (1882-1942).

S/N **16902**

An Italian serio-comic map of Europe during the Great War

86   Anonymous.

L'Europa nel 1915.

Milan: Luigi Ronchi di Candido Varoli, 1915. Chromolithograph, sheet 450 x 650mm. Binding folds reinforced, small repairs.

An Italian satirical map of Europe, with caricatures for the countries at war. France is a cockerel pecking the nose of the German dachshund, whose picklehelm is being punched by a long-legged British sailor. Austria howls with pain as its hind leg is crushed by the Russian steamroller driven by a grinning polar bear, and he is stabbed in the back by a Serbian bayonet.

Partly based on the 'Hark Hark' map by Johnson Riddle, this version seems to date to before the Treaty of London brought Italy into the war in May 1915; a later version has the placid Italian shown here clubbing the Austrian dog with the butt of his rifle.

See SOUCACOS: Satirical Maps p.216-7 for later issue.

S/N **17606**

The Appetite of the German Octopus

L'APPÉTIT DE LA PIEUVRE

87   ROBIDA, Albert.

L'Appétit de la Peuvre.

Paris, c.1914. Chromolithograph. Sheet 360 x 260mm. Wear to edges.

A French satire on the aggressively expansionist policies of Germany, depicting the German Eagle with octopus tentacles enveloping the world.

Robida worked for the 'La Caricature' magazine between 1880 and 1892, appearing in 650 issues, often on the cover. As well as his caricature work he was also a visionary: his sketches of war depict guided missiles and poison gas. Another sketch showed a mountaineer enjoying the view while listening to his 'phono-opéragraphe', with cables connected to his ears.

S/N **17542**

A socialist protest poster after the 1974 military coup in Portugal

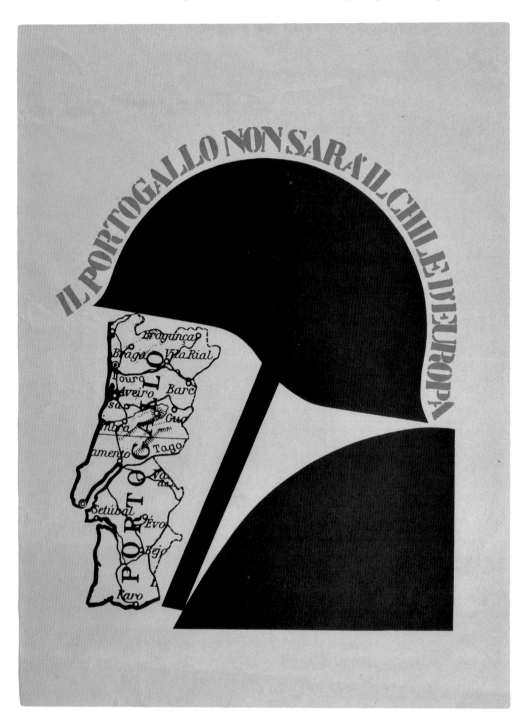

88   Anonymous.

Il Portogallo non sara' il Chile d'Europa.

Italian, c.1974. Lithograph, printed in black and red. Sheet 410 x 305mm.

A poster with the head of a soldier wearing a helmet, his face made from a map of Portugal.

Above is the anti-fascist slogan 'Portugal will not be the Chile of Europe'; this was the slogan of the 'Carnation Revolution' which overthrew the authoritarian regime of the Estado Novo in April 1974. The hope was that the coup wasn't going to emulate Augusto Pinochet's coup of 1973, which saw a thousand executions in the first six months, the abolition of civil liberties and 500% inflation in the first year. Instead Portugal evolved into a democratic country.

S/N **17591**

BORDERS, CARTOUCHES & VIGNETTES

Below is a random selection of maps picked to illustrate the full gamut of map illustration.

Mercator's famous map of the Arctic

89 MERCATOR, Gerard.

Septentrionalium Terrarum descriptio.

Amsterdam: Jodocus Hondius, 1606, Latin text edition. Coloured. 365 x 390mm. Margins rebuilt at bottom corners.

The first map of the Arctic Circle, with both the North Pole and Magnetic North depicted as rocky islands. Mercator has included the latest voyages in search of the North West and North East Passages, marking the discoveries of Frobisher and Davis around Greenland. Within the roundels of the decorative borders are maps of the Shetlands, Faeroes and the mythical island of Frisland.

This example is from the first edition of the Mercator atlas published by Jodocus Hondius, and is the first issue of the second state, which improves the outline of Novaya Zemlya, making it one island, and reduces the size of one of the polar islands to allow the inclusion of Spitzbergen.

A classic decorative map.

BURDEN: 88; KOEMAN: Me 15.

S/N **17614**

The only original map in Pitt's 'English Atlas'

90 PITT, Moses.

A Map of the North-Pole and the Parts Adjoining.

Oxford: Moses Pitt, 1680. Coloured. 460 x 590mm.

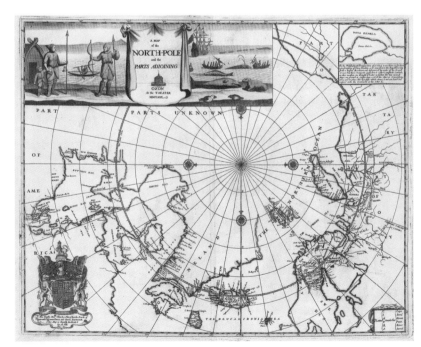

A scarce map of the Arctic Circle, with the title on a curtain, with portraits of Lapplanders and a whaling scene. On the map the mythical island of Frisland is marked, as is a strait through Greenland, placed there instead of Canada by Martin Frobisher, who had been confused by the non-existence of Frisland. Further west the discoveries of the English explorers looking for the North West Passage are shown.

Bottom left are the arms of Charles FitzCharles (1657-80), the son of Charles II, which consists of his father's arms with a baton sinister vair overall, signifying illegitimacy. He died of dysentery defending Tangier, which had been part of his father's dowry when marrying the Portuguese princess Catherine of Braganza in 1662.

S/N **17805**

The English and Dutch colonies in America with an early view of New York

91   DANCKERTS, Justus.

Novi Belgii Novaeque Angliae nec non Pennsylvaniae et Partis Virginiae Tabula.

Amsterdam, c.1690. Original colour. 470 x 550mm. The finest original colour we have seen on this map.

A scarce map, showing the eastern seaboard of America from Chesapeake Bay north to Pennobscot, with the as-yet unexplored St Lawrence River running across the top. Vignette animals include turkeys, beavers and bears and a Mohawk, based on the De Bry engravings, fills the middle left edge. Bottom right is a version of the Blaeu view of 'Nieuw Amsterdam', regarded as the earliest published view of New York.

First published c. 1673, this third and last state has been updated to reflect the new status quo, in which the English dominance is acknowledged: the view has been renamed 'Nieuw Yorck', and Philadelphia, founded 1682, is marked.

BURDEN: 434.

S/N **16467**

A monumental wall map of the Pacific and America

92   CHÂTELAIN, Henri Abraham.

Carte très curieuse de la Mer du Sud, contenant des Remarques Nouvelles et très utiles non seulement sur des Ports et Îles de cette Mer, mais aussy sur les principaux Pays de l'Amerique tant Septentrionale que Méridionale en a été faite.

Amsterdam, 1719. Four sheets conjoined, total 830 x 1410mm. A superb example.

A large map of the western hemisphere, centred on the Americas but showing the coasts of Western Europe & Africa on the right, China & Japan on the left, with the partial outlines of Australia & New Zealand. California is shown as an island, but the north of the island has lighter shading to suggest doubt, as has the western half of the Terra del Fuego. Jesso and Companies Land are also shown above Japan, but two large vignettes of beavers cover the gap between Asia and America. Other vignettes include portraits of the most important explorers; plans of Panama, Acapulco, Mexico City & Havana; depictions of mining, panning for gold, sugar milling, a cod fishery and human sacrifice.

The map was included in Chatelain's seven-volume 'Atlas Historique', published between 1705 and 1720. This encyclopedic work was devoted to the history and genealogy of the continents, with a text, written by Nicolas Gueudeville, on topics including geography, cosmography, topography, heraldry, and ethnography.

GOSS: Mapping of North America 52, 'a veritable pictorial encyclopaedia of the western hemisphere'.

S/N **17821**

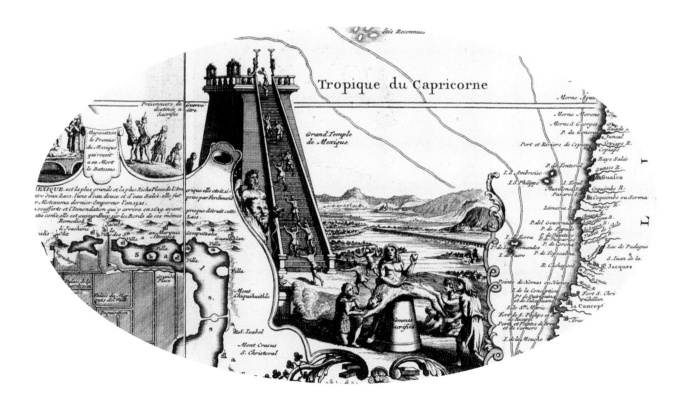

CARTE TRES CURIEUSE DE LA MER DU SUD, CONTENANT DES REMARQUES NOUV..

Mais auffy fur les principaux Pays de l'Amerique tant Septentrionale que Meridionale, Avec les Noms & la R..

S ET TRES UTILES NON SEULEMENT SUR LES PORTS ET ILES DE CETTE MER,

Voyageurs par qui la decouverte en a été faite. Le tout pour *l'intelligence Des Dissertations suivantes*

TERRE DE LABRADOR, par les Espagnols.
NOUVELLE BRETAGNE, par les Anglois.
ESTOTILANDE, par les Danois.
CANADA SEPTENTRIONAL, par les François.

SAGUENAY

MER DU

NORD

MER DU CANCER

Tropique du Cancer

SUD

AMERIQUE

PAYS DES AMAZONES

BRESIL

MERIDIONALE

Tropique du Capricorne

TUCUMAN

TERRE MAGELLANIQUE

Patagons

MER DU SUD

EQUATEUR OU LIGNE EQUINOCTIAL

GOLFE DE MEXIQUE

ISLES ANTILLES OU DU VENT

TERRE FERME

NOUVELLE GRENADE FERME

GUIANE ou GUAIANE

COSTES DU BRESIL

RIO DE LA PLATA

BAYE DE RIO JANEIRO

ISLANDE
ESCOSE
IRLANDE
ANGLETERRE
FRANCE
ESPAGNE
MEDITERRANÉE
DETROIT DE GIBRALTAR

BARBARIE

Rª D'ALGER   Rª DE TUNIS
Rª DE FEZ   Rª MAROC ET TAFILET
Rª DE MAROC
Rª DE TAFILET
Rª DE SENEGA

LE SARA OU DESERT DE BARBARIE

Les Isles Açores ou Tercere

Les Isles Canaries

Isles du Cap Vert

NIGRITIE

HAUTE GUINEE

Rª DE BENIN

BASSE GUINEE OU ETATS

OCEAN

CAFRERIE DES CAFRES

MERIDIONAL

Tropique du Capricorne

CAP DE BONNE ESPERANCE

Royaume de Loango
Royaume de Congo
Royaume d'Angla
DE CONGO
Royaume de Bengola

Danet's maps of the Continents with fine borders

93 DANET, Guillaume.

L'Amerique Meridionale et Septentrionale...

Paris: L.C. Desnos, 1760. Original colour. 480 x 690mm. Centre fold restored, printer's crease in bottom border.

Map of the Americas decorated with a large baroque title cartouche and a decorative border containing roundel portraits and the signs of the zodiac. In the north west is the fictitious 'Mer de l'Ouest' with a presumed channel leading to Hudson's Bay. Bottom right is an inset showing the supposed Russian discoveries in the North Pacific as reported by Joseph de l'Isle.

Danet was the son-in-law and successor of De Fer, and republished many of his maps These maps were only occasionally published in composite atlases and are therefore quite scarce.

S/N **16630**

94 DANET, Guillaume.

L'Asie Dressée Sur de nouveaux Memoires Assujetis aux observations Astronomiq. Corrigée et Augmentée...

Paris: Louis Charles Desnos, 1760. Original colour. 515 x 725mm.

The border containing the arms of Asian countries (including Cyprus), with the left and bottom borders dedicated to the Emperor of Japan and his nobles. On the map the semi-mythical land of Jesso joins Kamchatka, and the title cartouche hides the eastern end of 'Terre de Compagnie' in the North Pacific.

S/N **16494**

95 DANET, Guillaume.

L'Afrique Dressée Sur Les Relations & nouvelles decouvertes de differens Voyageurs Conformes aux observatio.ns Astronomiques.

Paris: Louis Charles Desnos, 1760. Original colour. 490 x 720mm.

A large and rare map of Africa, not listed in either Tooley or Norwich. It is decorated with a large allegorical cartouche featuring a female Europe and a male Africa, both holding manacles, representing the valuable slaves trade. The engraved border is filled with 4 armorials, European and Asian as well as African, interspersed with shells.

S/N **16496**

96 DANET, Guillaume.

L'Europe Divisée dans ses Principaux Etats Subdivisés en leurs Principales Provinces...

Paris: L.C. Desnos, 1760. Original colour. 715 x 740mm. Centre fold restored, pair of printer's creases in bottom border.

A French map of Europe decorated with a large baroque title cartouche and a decorative border containing the arms of countries, states and towns throughout the continent.

S/N **16587**

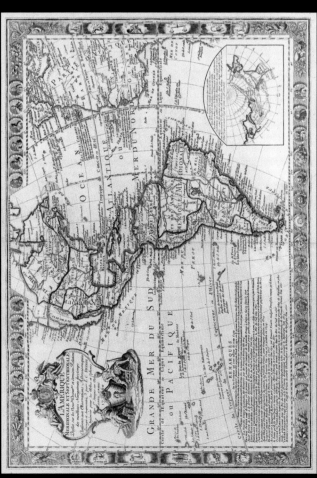

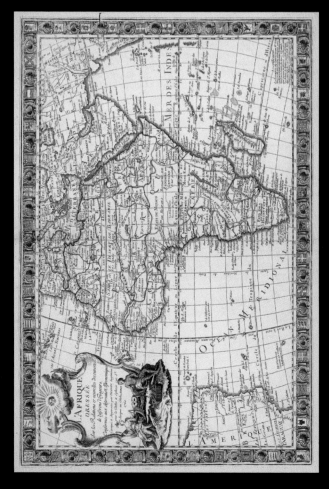

A two-sheet wall map of the United States

97   COLTON, J.H.

Map of the United States of America, The British Provinces, Mexico, the West Indies and Central America, with part of New Granada and Venezuela.

New York: J.H. Colton, 1853. Steel engraving with original hand colour. Two sheets conjoined, total 865 x 1075mm. A pristine example.

A brightly-coloured map of the United States surrounded by a decorative border of vines and grapes linking vignette scenes. Above the title is another vignette featuring a bald eagle in front of a port, with a locomotive and a paddle steamer. Two other insets show the North Atlantic and the trans-Panama railway.

On the map Oregon Territory is still coloured in its pre-1853 entirety, prior to the creation of Washington Territory, although 'Washington' is written across the top half.

Most of these large Colton maps were issued dissected and laid on linen, so to find an uncut example such as this is unusual.

S/N **17402**

The first printed map of the county of Devon

98 SAXTON, Christopher.

Devoniae Comitat, Rerumquae omnium in eodem memorabilium recens, vers pticularisq. Descriptio.

London, 1575-c.1579. Original colour lightly refreshed. 400 x 450mm. Narrow top margin, minor repairs, laid on linen.

A rare example of the first published state of Saxton's map of Devon, engraved in 1575 by Remigius Hogenberg (brother of the more famous Frans Hogenberg) for Saxton's county atlas of 1579. The arms above the title are those of Thomas Seckford (1515-87), who commissioned Saxton's survey, with those of Queen Elizabeth I top left. On the map towns, rivers and hills are marked, but it was not until nearly a century later that roads were routinely shown on county maps.

Saxton's copperplates had a long career: after being eclipsed by John Speed's atlas of 1611, the plates were re-engraved and re-issued in 1642 by William Web. Although most of the other plates were still being printed as late as 1770, the Devon plate had either been lost or destroyed by the 1689 Lea edition.

BATTEN: 1.

S/N **15840**

The first printed map of Westmorland and Cumberland

99   SAXTON, Christopher.

Westmorlandiae et Cumberlandiae Comit. nova vera et Elaborata descriptio. An° Dni 1576.

London, 1576-c.1579. Original colour lightly refreshed. 395 x 450mm. A few nicks in the margins.

The first published state of Saxton's map of both Cumberland and Westmorland, engraved in 1576 by Augustine Ryther for Saxton's county atlas of 1579. Top right are the arms of Queen Elizabeth, with the arms of Thomas Seckford (1515 -87, who commissioned Saxton's survey) underneath, balanced with the strapwork title cartouche and a pair of compasses on the scale on the left. On the map towns, rivers and hills are marked, but it was not until nearly a century later that roads were routinely shown on county maps.

Saxton's copperplates had a long career: after being eclipsed by John Speed's atlas of 1611, the plates were re-engraved and re-issued in 1642 by William Web; most of the other plates were still being printed as late as 1770.

S/N **17807**

Map of Surrey and Sussex from Drayton's fantastical 'Poly-Olbion'

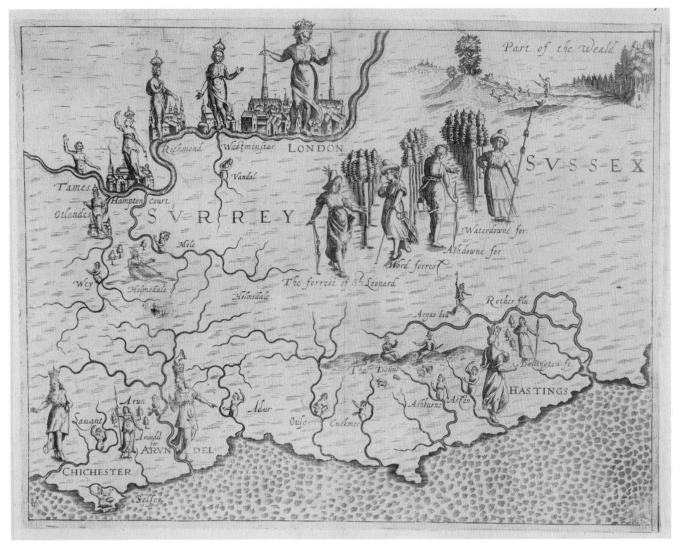

100 DRAYTON, Michael.

[Svrrey; London; Svssex.]

London, 1612. 255 x 330mm.

A very decorative map of Surrey and Sussex, ignoring political boundaries and instead focusing on natural features, with hills and rivers populated by allegorical figures. Major towns are marked. London; Westminster; Hampton Court; Richmond; Arundel; Chichester; Hastings and part of the Weald are shown as well as the Rivers Thames, Arun, Rother and Mole.

Michael Drayton (1563-1631), a prominent poet, is believed to have started work on his 'Poly-Olbion' in 1598. This epic topographical poem, divided into thirty songs written in alexandrine couplets, ran to nearly 15,000 lines of verse. Each song described one, two or three counties, describing their topography, traditions and histories. The First Part was published in 1612, with eighteen maps probably engraved by William Hole (who signed the frontispiece).

Drayton had been a favourite of Queen Elizabeth's court, but was not so popular with James I. Perhaps to rectify this the 'Poly-Olbion' was dedicated to Henry, Prince of Wales, but Henry died in 1612, the year of publication. The work did not sell well, and it was not until 1622 that Drayton could find a publisher for the second part, which contained ten more maps. Drayton intended to compose a further part to cover Scotland, but no part of this work is known to have survived. Despite these setbacks Drayton was still prominent enough to be buried in Poets' Corner in Westminster Abbey when he died in 1631. It was only posthumously that the Poly-Olbion became a literary classic.

S/N **14044**

An extremely rare prospect of Bristol

101   MILLERD, James.

The Citty of Bristoll.

Bristol: James Millerd, & London: John Overton & Thomas Wall, 1673. Two sheets conjoined, total 305 x 705mm. Repaired tear.

An elevated prospect of Bristol from the south, with Aston and Clifton on the left horizon, the Royal Fort in the centre and Horsfield & Ashley on the right. The title is on a banderole in the centre, with the arms of two Earls of Bristol underneath, with space for a third. In the top corners are the arms of Charles II and his Queen, Catherine of Braganza, with the arms of the City of Bristol and the Society of the Merchants of Bristol underneath. In the bottom corners are two verses in Latin, keys of Churches and other landmarks. Along the bottom is an advert for Millerd's four-sheet map of Bristol. Just above that is an oddity: a dedication to the major and aldermen of the city has had curtains engraved over the top, probably because Millerd did not receive the civic recognition he felt was his due. The example in the Bristol Museums Galleries has the same feature.

Millerd's three works were first published between 1670 and 1677, the other two being maps of Bristol. He is also recorded as being a mercer and a 'Guardian of the Poor', appointed to administer the poor laws in the city.

WORMS & BAYNTON-WILLIAMS: British Map Engravers, p. 450.

S/N **16868**

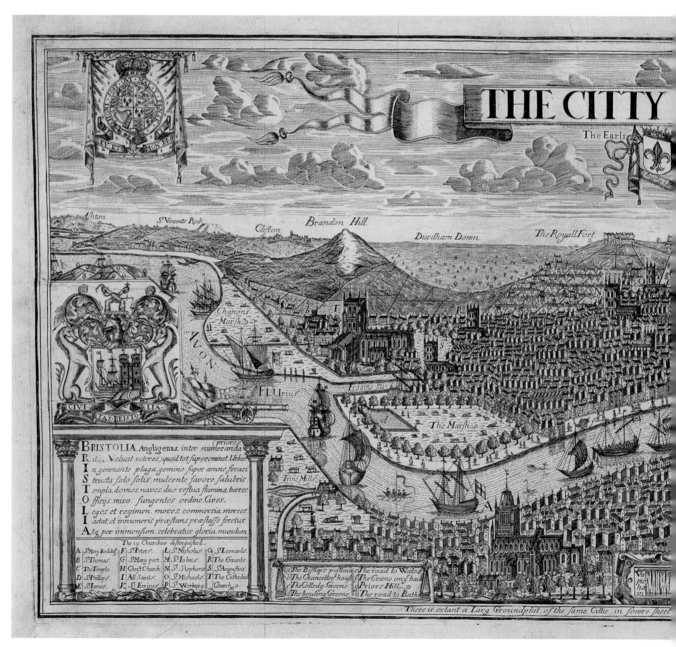

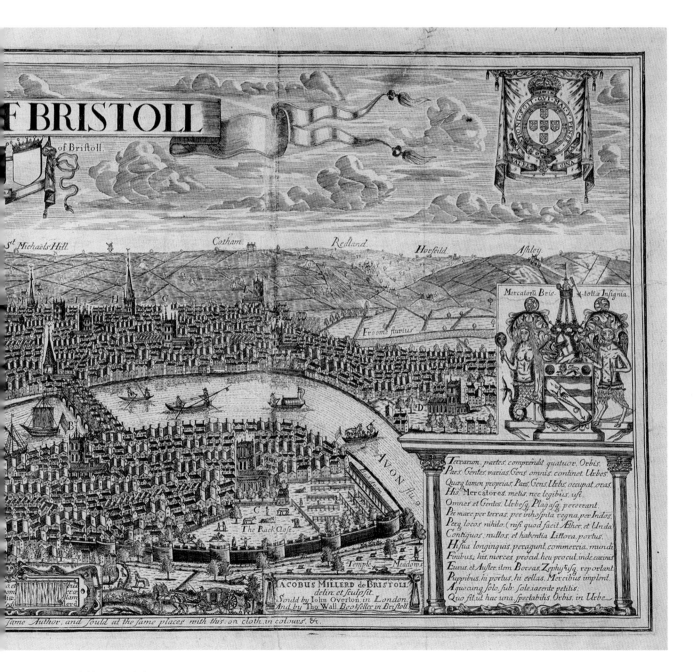

A scarce two-sheet map of Oxfordshire

102   OLIVER, John.

Oxfordshire Actualy Survey'd &c. Humbly Dedicated to the R.t Reverend Father in God George L.d Bishop of Bristol Dean of Christchurch & Lord Almoner to his Majesty.

London: Philip Overton, 1715. Coloured. Two sheets conjoined, total 585 x 900mm. Some restoration.

A majestic map of Oxfordshire, orientated with north to the right, with a decorative title cartouche; a prospect of Oxford from the east; a depiction of a Romaic mosaic at Stonesfield, featuring Bacchus riding a panther (since destroyed); and elevations of Blenheim Palace and Bridge, the Radcliffe Camera and 'The Publick Schools in Oxford'.

This is one of three two-sheet maps engraved for the abortive 'Atlas Anglicanus', a large folio county atlas, to be created in partnership with John Seller and Richard Palmer. After the project collapsed Overton bought the plates for this map; Oliver's name only remains as engraver.

John Oliver (1616?-1701), a builder, architect and glass-painter as well as being a surveyor, engraver and publisher, married one of John Speed's grand-daughters. He became official surveyor of the City of London in 1668, two years after the Great Fire; the resultant map was published by Seller c.1680. Oliver associated with Robert Hooke and makes several appearances in his diary, in which Hooke calls him variously a rascal, villain, dog and devil; however this did not stop the pair visiting Bartholomew Fair together to see a tiger. In 1686 he became Master Mason to James II.

WORMS & BAYNTON-WILLIAMS: British Map Engravers, p.501-2.

S/N **14550**

Fine plan of the naval dockyard at Sheerness, Kent

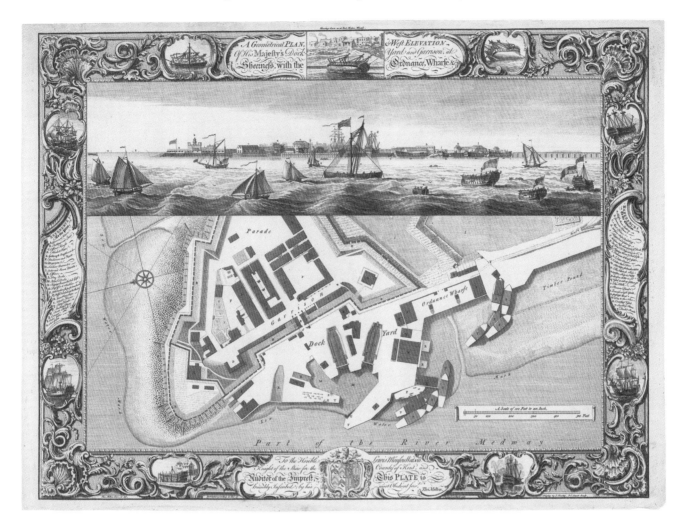

103   MILTON, Thomas.

A Geometrical Plan, & West Elevation of His Majesty's Dock-Yard and Garrison, at Sheerness; with the Ordnance Wharf &c.

London, 1755. 495 x 660mm.

A plan and prospect of the famous naval dockyard, finely engraved by P.C.Canot after Milton, both with a 24-point key. Around the whole is a rococo frame-like border containing vignette scenes of the works of the dockyard, drawn by John Clevely, a shipwright whose son James Clevely jnr is famous for his painting of the death of Captain Cook.

Sheerness Naval Dockyard was founded by Samuel Pepys in 1663 to improve the defences on the eastern coast of England, at a time the Dutch were a threat. Indeed the Dutch admiral De Ruyter actually occupied the town of Sheerness briefly in 1667. Consequently the defences were constantly improved, including a remodel by John Rennie, opened in 1823.

S/N **8492**

A decorative wall map of England & Wales

104   SEATON, Robert.

This New Map of England and Wales, with the Adjacent Countries, Compiled by Surveyors in the Ordnance Department, is Respectfully Dedicated to the King, by his Majestys Most Obedient Servant and Geographer, Robert Seaton.

London, James Neele & Co, c.1835. Fine original colour. Dissected and laid on linen as issued, total 1170 x 940mm, with slipcase.

A detailed map of England and Wales in fine original colour, with regional boundaries, roads, railways, settlements and topography marked. Dedicated to William IV, it has a large vignette of Windsor Castle above the title, views of Westminster Abbey, York Minster, St Paul's and Canterbury Cathedral in the four corners, and 28 portraits of British worthies in the borders. Along the top are soldiers, including Marlborough and Wellington; down the left are politicians, including Fox, Pitt and Canning; down the right are intellectuals, including Shakespeare, Newton, Pope, Byron and Burns.

S/N **10838**

A wall map of Scotland in strong original colour

105   KITCHIN, Thomas.

A New and Complete Map of Scotland, And Islands thereto belonging; From Actual Surveys, The Shires properly Divided, and Subdivided, the Forts lately erected & Roads of Communication, or Military Ways; Carried on by His Majesty's Command; The Times when, and Places where the most remarkable Battles have been fought. Likewise the Roman Camps, Forts, Walls, & Military Ways; The Danish Camps, & Forts; Also the Seats of the Nobility in each Shire distinguished, with several other remarkable Places, that Occur in the History of Scotland.

London: Laurie & Whittle, c.1794. Original colour. Four sheets conjoined, dissected and laid on linen as issued, total 1200 x 1015mm, folded into contemporary marbled slipcase. Some surface wear in unprinted areas.

A large and colourful map of Scotland, first published in the 1760s by Carington Bowles, at the end of the project to build Military Roads across Scotland. It was started by General George Wade in 1724 because of the continuing Jacobite threat and ended with the death of Major William Caulfeild in 1767.

On this example the original publisher's name has been erased but, unusually, Laurie and Whittle have not added their names. The map most often appears in atlases in two sections, with outline colour; full-colour examples such as this are uncommon.

S/N **17433**

Early map of the roads from London to Oxford, illustrated with the waywiser cartouche

106   OGILBY, John.

The Road from London to Aberistwith...

London, c.1675, second state. Coloured. 330 x 445mm.

The first sheet of three showing the route from London to Aberystwyth, beginning in the centre of the City, passing through Uxbridge, Beaconsfield and High Wycombe, ending at Islip, but with a spur to Oxford.

Plate 1 from Ogilby's 'Britannia', the first national road-atlas of any country in Western Europe. It was composed of maps of seventy-three major roads and cross-roads, presented as trompe-l'œil scrolls, each with a decorative title cartouche, this being one of only four featuring the way-wiser. It was the first English atlas on a uniform scale, at one inch to a mile, and the 'mile' Ogilby used became the national standard, the statute mile of 1,760 yards. Ogilby claimed that 26,600 miles of roads were surveyed in the course of preparing the atlas, on foot using the surveyor's wheel depicted in the cartouche, but only about 7,500 were actually depicted in print. It was only after the 'Britannia' that roads started being shown on county maps.

Second state, with plate number bottom right.

S/N **16319**

Superbly-decorated map of Ogilby's roads of England and Wales

107   WILLDEY, George.

The Roads of England According to Mr Ogilby's Survey.

London: George Willdey, c.1713. Contemporary colour refreshed. 590 x 595mm. Repairs to folds, laid on archival paper.

A scarce separate-issue map of England and Wales arranged to show the roads as surveyed for John Ogilby's 'Britannia'. To make the detail marked on the roads clear (for example the distances between towns) the geographical outline of the country is distorted, fitting into a circle. Bottom left there is no attempt to show the Cornish peninsula, yet Land's End is marked. The rich borders are decorated with acanthus leaves, with roundels containing armorials.

The map is unusual in that it was printed from two plates, a circular plate, 525mm in diameter, for the map and a second plate for the border. As this border has no distinct 'up', examples exist where the border is rotated in relation to the map into all four cardinals. This example is rotated 90° clockwise to the illustration in Shirley. The map can also be found without the border.

Ogilby's 'Britannia' was the world's first printed road atlas, published 1675, a hugely-influential publication; soon his roads started appearing on British county maps, and, nearly forty years later, Ogilby's work was still being used.

SHIRLEY: Willdey 1, 'striking road map'; this second state, not listed in Shirley, has apparent 'crossing-out' lines through Willdey's imprint.

S/N **16276**

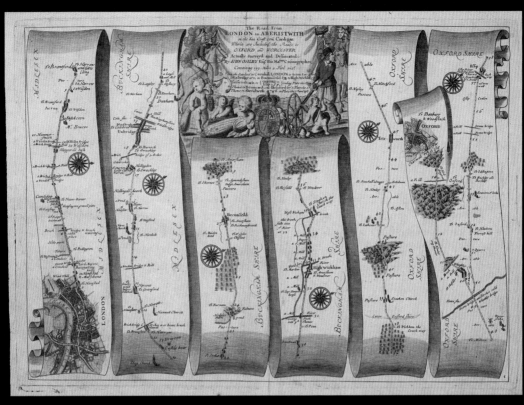

Item 106

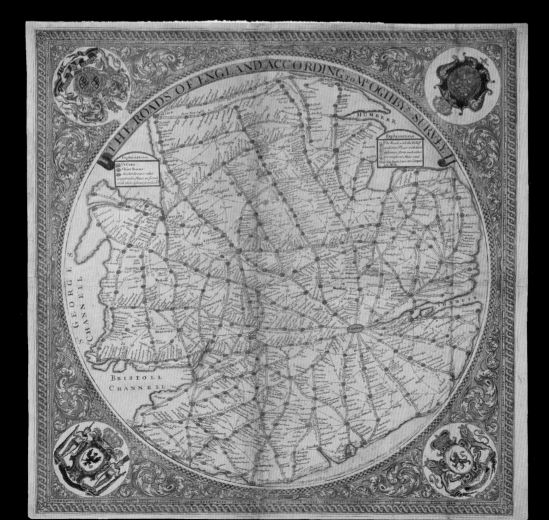

The first available printed map of London

108   BRAUN, Georg & HOGENBERG, Frans.

Londinum Feracissimi Angliae Regni Metropolis.

Koln: c.1574. Coloured. 330 x 490mm.

The earliest town plan of London to survive, a 'map-view' with the major buildings shown in profile, and no consideration for perspective. It was published in the 'Civitates Orbis Terrarum', the first series of printed town plans, inspired by the success of the 'Theatrum', the atlas compiled by Abraham Ortelius. This example is from the second state of the plate, issued two years after the first, with the spelling 'West Muster' and the addition of the Royal Exchange.

The plan was engraved by Frans Hogenberg, copied from a 15-or-20-sheet printed map, probably commissioned by the merchants of the Hanseatic League, who had significant commercial interests in England. For over two centuries they had enjoyed tax and customs concessions in the trade of wool and finished cloth, allowing them to control that trade in Colchester and other cloth-making centres. Their base in the City was the Steelyard (derived from 'Stalhof'), named 'Stiliyards' by the side of the Thames on this map and described in the text panel lower right. They purchased the building in 1475; part of the deal was their obligation to maintain Bishopsgate, the gate through the city walls that led to their interests in East Anglia. The rump cities of the Hanseatic League sold the building in 1853 and it is now the site of Cannon Street Station.

The map must have been drawn fifteen years or so before publication: in the centre is the Norman St. Paul's Cathedral, with the spire that was hit by lighting and destroyed in 1561 and not replaced before the Great Fire of London destroyed the building in 1666.

HOWGEGO: 2 (2).

S/N **17284**

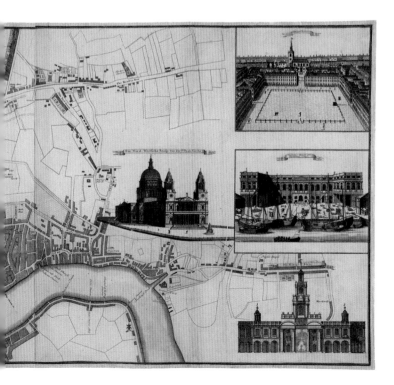

A fine three-sheet map of Georgian London

109 HOMANN HEIRS.

Urbium Londini et West-Monasterii nec non Suburbii Southwark accurata Ichnographia… 1736.

Nuremberg, 1736. Original colour with additions. Three sheets conjoined, total 520 x 1720mm.

A large and very decorative town plan of London, showing from Grosvenor Square and Buckingham House in the west to Stepney Church in the east, Clerkenwell in the north and Southwark in the south. Many of the most important buildings are shown in profile, and, sixty years after the event, the extent of the losses of the Great Fire of London are still marked. A large title cartouche with the Royal arms of George II completes this very striking map.

This map often appears just as a two-sheet map. The right sheet here, half of which is taken up with a view of St James's Square and elevations of St Paul's, the Royal Exchange and the Custom House, was only included in a deluxe edition.

HOWGEGO: 81.

S/N **16076**

London during the Great Exhibition of 1851

110   TALLIS, John.

Tallis's Illustrated Plan of London and its Environs in Commemoration of the Great Exhibition of Industry of All Nations, 1851.

London, John Tallis & Co., 1851. Original Colour. Dissected and laid on linen as issued, total 550 x 750mm.

A detailed map of London, extending to Hammersmith in the west, clockwise to Cricklewood, Hampstead, Stamford Hill, Leytonstone, Greenwich, Peckham, Battersea Rise and Parson's Green. Around the edges are 49 views of buildings including, of course, the 'Crystal Palace' of the Great Exhibition in Hyde Park.

HYDE: 22.

S/N **16906**

A quad royal pictorial map of London's Underground

111   GILL, Leslie MacDonald.

In The Heat Of The Summer You Will Find Me Cool In The Cold Of The Winter Find Me Warm Come Down Underground You've Bought Your Ticket? Your Health Man I'm Thinking No Longer 'Twill Stick It For Cheapness Celerity What Else Can Compare You Are Fed Up Above Feed Below On Our Fare'

London: Underground Electric Railways Company of London, 1922. 1015 x 1270mm. Some wear.

A map of Central London showing the Underground stations, drawn by Leslie MacDonald Gill, in the style of his famous 'Wonderground' map of 1914, but with new details. It does not extend as far north or south, but instead has nine armorials (the eight principal London boroughs and a ninth for a rabbit, returning to the Alice theme) and a decorative scroll containing the title. Bottom right is his signature and a further text: 'Will the tired traveller wearisomely realise that this map is meticulously accurate (with exceptions), that it has been punctiliously delineated to the scale of six inches to the mile and that its merry quips are well meant even when unintelligible'.

Leslie MacDonald Gill (1884-1947), younger brother of Eric Gill, specialised in graphic design in the Arts and Crafts style. His most important commission was from the Imperial War Graves Commission, designing the script used on Commission headstones and war memorials, including the 'Thiepval Memorial to the Missing of the Somme'. He produced a number of maps, two of which appeared in the British Museum exhibition 'Magnificent Maps' in 2010: 'The Wonderground Map of London' (1914) & 'Tea Revives the World' (1940).

S/N **16850**

A large and decorative plan of Paris published the year of the Battle of Waterloo

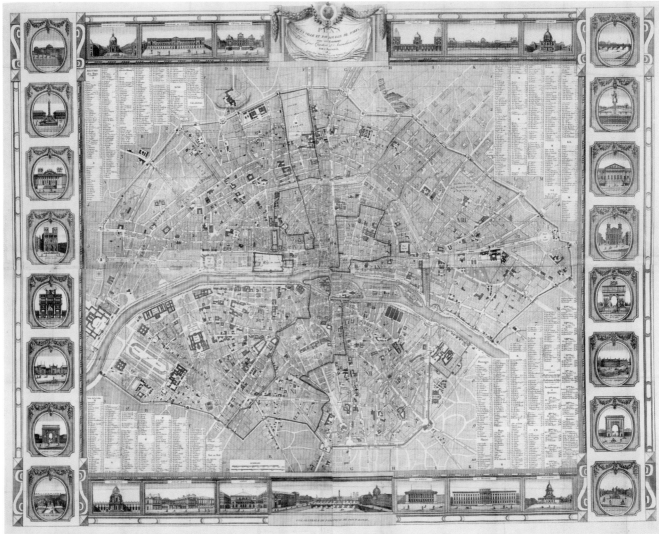

112   BONNISEL, J.

Plan de la Ville et Faubourgs de Paris, avec ses Monuments Divisé par Quartiers et Arrondissments. 1815.

Paris: Jean, 1815. Original outline colour. Four sheets conjoined, total 950 x 1200mm. A fine example.

A large and detailed plan of Paris, decorated with 29 views and elevations of important buildings and monuments in the side panels, including the Louvre Museum, the Arc de Triomphe, the Petit Palais Musee des Beaux-Arts, the Notre Dame Cathedral and the Tuileries Palace.

A detailed key lists streets, bridges, arrondissements, cemeteries and even slaughterhouses, locating them on the map using a coordinate system.

S/N **16861**

A very scarce plan of Dublin with vignettes

113   HEFFERNAN, Daniel Edward.

Dublin in 1861.

Dublin: Heffernan, 1861. Steel engraving on india. 630 x 940mm, wide margins. Some restoration, card backing reinforced with canvas.

A detailed plan of Dublin with the important buildings shown in elevation, with oval prospects of the city in the four corners, two lists of events and a border of 32 oval views of buildings.

The artist was an engineer, surveyor and valuator of Dublin, active in the mid-nineteenth century. He published similar plans of Bray and Wicklow and supplied 18 engravings for 'The Official Railway Hand-book' to Bray, including some that decorate this plan.

http://architectureireland.ie/daniel-edward-heffernans-map-of-dublin-1861

S/N **17296**

A 'board game' map of Europe

114 SPOONER, William.

The Travellers; or A Tour Through Europe; with Improvements and Additions.

London: William Spooner, 1842. Lithographic folding map with hand colour. Dissected and laid on linen as issued, 500 x 630mm. Some wear.

A 'goose game' map of Europe, illustrated with vignettes of the most important cities of Europe, the Near East and North Africa. Where the cities thin out, for example in the steppes of Russia, there are vignettes of sledging, arctic animals and whale fishing.

According to the Victoria and Albert Museum's catalogue, 'Five players take the parts of The Travellers, who are from different nations, Austria, Sweden, Russia, Prussia and England. They must make their way to their respective capital cities each starting from a different city in Africa, or on the shore of the Mediterranean Sea. This game is played with a teetotum or spinner with four sides marked N, S, E, W representing the directions they must move in'.

S/N **16865**

Early 18th century plan of St Petersburg

115   HOMANN, Johann Baptist.

Topographische Vorstellung der Neuen Russischen Haupt-Residenz und See-Stadt St. Petersburg...

Nuremberg, c.1721. Original colour. 500 x 595mm.

One of the most decorative of Homann's town plans, dedicated to the city's founder Peter the Great. His image can be seen in the huge title cartouche, surrounded by allegorical figures representing the arts and sciences he nurtured, including ship-building (which he studied in a shipyard in Deptford), printing & geography. A second map shows the position of the city in the mouth of the River Neva, and a vignette view shows the fortified island 'Crohn Schlot' protecting the city's approaches.

S/N **16441**

A wall map of the British Flanders Campaign of the French Revolutionary War

116   KITCHIN, Thomas.

A New Map of the Netherlands or Low Countries, with the South Part of the Provinces of Holland, Utrecht, & Gelders, and the whole of Zeeland.

London: Laurie & Whittle, 1794. Original full body colour. Four sheets, dissected and laid on linen as issued. Total 980 x 1210mm. A few signs of use.

A folding map of the Austrian Netherlands, published during the Flanders Campaign of the French Revolutionary War. The large vignette above the title shows the Siege of Valenciennes in 1793, in which the British and Austrians under Prince Frederick, Duke of York and Albany, took the city from the Republicans. Frederick, shown here on horseback, waving his hat, was welcomed by the French population, who tore down the Republican Tricolour and proclaimed him King of France. Unfortunately this was one of the few successes of the campaign: the following year the Coalition was forced to retreat, reaching Bremen in Hanover in the spring of 1795, leaving the Dutch Republic in the hands of France.

This is an unusual presentation of this map: normally it is found in Laurie & Whittle atlases with basic outline colour, so this example seems to have been published in the short period of Allied success, possibly for a serving officer.

S/N **15434**

An 18th century plan of Venice

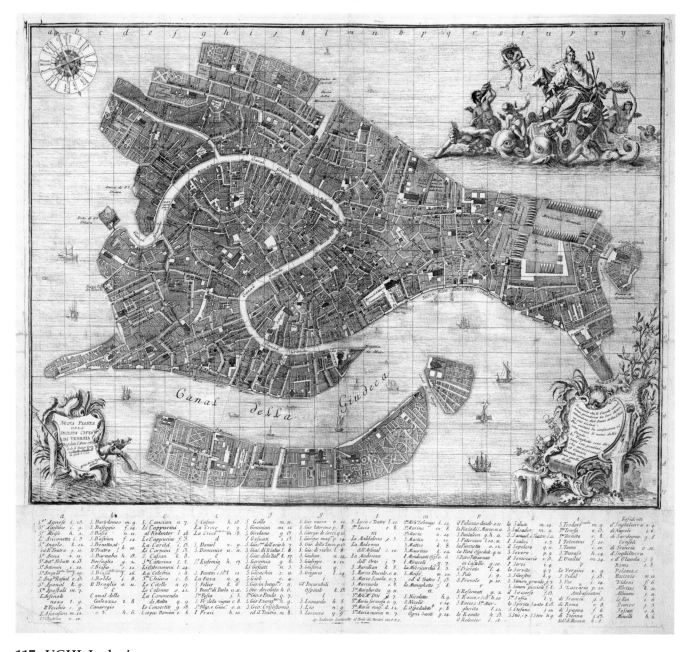

117 UGHI, Ludovico.

Nuova Pianta dell'Inclita Citta di Venezia Regolata l'Anno 1787.

Venice, Ludovico Furlanetto, 1787. 515 x 680mm, with separately printed key pasted underneath. Minor repairs to folds.

A reduction of Ughi's 8-sheet map of 1725, this version first published in 1747. This is an example of the second state, with a title and date added in the scale cartouche, and a grid engraved over the map, referred to by the extensive key printed on a separate sheet and attached under the map.

There are three more states known, the last in 1829.

MORETTI: Venetia, 188, state 2 of 5.

S/N **17819**

An early prospect of Budapest

118   BRAUN, Georg & HOGENBERG, Frans.

Buda Citerioris Hungariae Caput Regni Avita sedes, Vulgo Ofen.

Cologne, 1617, French text verso, coloured, 320 x 475mm, good margins.

A splendid view of the cities of Buda and Pest (modern-day Budapest) engraved by Joris Hoefnagel, for the 'Civitates Orbis Terrarum', volume 6.

Buda is seen from across the Danube with its huge hilltop fortress and royal palace. On the opposite bank is the strongly fortified town of Pest, with a pontoon bridge linking the two. The engraving depicts the two towns during the period of Ottoman occupation, when Buda was the seat of the local Pasha.

The illustration in the foreground shows the Pasha with his delija (bodyguard) who wears feathers pierced through the skin of his scalp.

S/N **17365**

18th century map of Malta celebrating the Knights of Malta

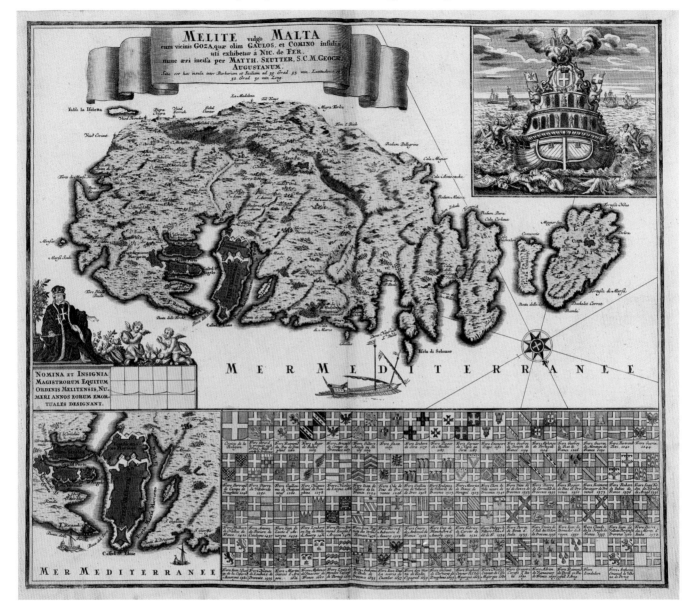

119 SEUTTER, Matthäus.

Melite vulgo Malta cum vicinis Goza, quæ olim Gaulos, et Comino insulis, uti exhibetur á Nic. De Fer.

Augsburg, c.1730. Original colour. 500 x 580mm. Very fine example.

A large and decorative map of Malta, orientated with north to the bottom right, with an inset map of Valletta, the arms of 64 Grand Masters of the Knights of Malta, and an allegorical scene representing the sea power of the Knights.

S/N **16116**

Classic 17th century Dutch map of Cyprus

120 BLAEU, Johannes.

Cyprus Insula.

Amsterdam, 1662, Latin edition. Fine original colour. 390 x 410mm, wide margins.

A famous map of Cyprus, with Famagusta, Nicosia and Limassol marked in red, published in Blaeu's monumental 11-volume 'Atlas Major'.

The large title cartouche depicts a famous story from Greek mythology; Aphrodite, seated in a shell being drawn across the sea to Cyprus by a pair of swans, is pricked with an arrow by her son Cupid, which causes her to fall in love with Adonis. Unfortunately he was killed by a boar.

ZACHARAKIS: 243, illus. pl.40; BANK OF CYPRUS: 66; SCUTARI (Comp): Sweet Land of Cyprus 51, 'perhaps the finest map of Cyprus'.

S/N **16535**

A superb 17th century plan of Venice

121 CORONELLI, Vincenzo Maria.

Citta di Venetia.

Venice, c.1693. Two sheets conjoined, total 490 x 770mm. Remargined at top, as usual with this large format plate.

A magnificent, large-scale bird's-eye view of Venice, surrounded by armorials of the Venetian nobility on a garland, the Venetian lion top centre. This is an example of the first state (of three), still with the date of 1693 in the dedication roundel.

This is a scarce map: it does not appear in all of Coronelli's atlases and the examples that did were often damaged because of the large height and width.

MORETTO: 114, first state of three, 'considered one of the most beautiful and appreciated Venetian maps'.

S/N **17736**

Celestial chart of Tycho Brahe's theories of the Universe

122 CELLARIUS, Andreas.

Planisphaerium Braheum, sive structura Mundi Totius, ex hypothesi Tychonis Brahei in plano delineata.

Amsterdam, Schenk & Valk, 1708. Original colour with additions, including gold highlights. 440 x 515mm.

A beautiful celestial chart depicting the 'planisphere of Brahe, or the structure of the universe following the hypothesis of Tycho Brahe drawn in a planar view'. The Danish Astronomer Tycho Brahe posited a Solar System merging the theories of Ptolemy and Copenicus, so that the Sun revolved around the earth, but the planets were bound to the Sun. Jupiter is shown with four moons. In the borders the title banners are held up by putti, and portraits of Brahe at his Hven observatory bottom right and probably Ptolemy bottom left.

This chart was published in the 'Atlas Coelestis; seu Harmonia Macrocosmica', the only celestial atlas to be produced in the Netherlands before the nineteenth century. It was a compilation of maps of the Ptolemaic universe and the more modern theories of Copernicus and Brahe, and remains the finest and most highly decorative celestial atlas ever produced. It was originally published by Jan Jansson in 1660: this chart comes from Schenk & Valk's reissue.

KOEMAN: Cel 3.

S/N **13526**

The world's construction according to Tycho Brahe

123   CELLARIUS, Andreas.

Scenographia compagis mundanae Brahea.

Amsterdam, Schenk & Valk, 1708. Original colour with additions, including gold highlights. 440 x 515mm.

'Scenography of the world's construction according to Brahe.' A fine celestial chart showing the world's eastern hemisphere, with the motions of the sun and planets and a band representing the Zodiac. The borders are filled with putti and allegorical figures holding scientific instruments.

KOEMAN: Cel 3.

S/N **13543**

A stunning pair of 18th century celestial hemispheres

124 DOPPELMAYR, Johann Gabriel.

Hemisphaerium Coeli Boreale. [&] Hemisphaerium Coeli Australe.

Nuremberg, Homann's Heirs, 1742. Original colour with additions. Two sheets, ea. c.485 x 580mm. Fine condition.

The Northern and Southern skies, divided into the Classical Constellations. In the corners are elevations of eight of the most important observatories of Europe, including Greenwich.

Most of the constellations depicted are still familiar today, but on the Southern sheet is 'Robur Carolinum' (Charles's Oak), introduced by Edmund Halley in 1678 but not one of the 88 constellations recognised today.

S/N **16646**

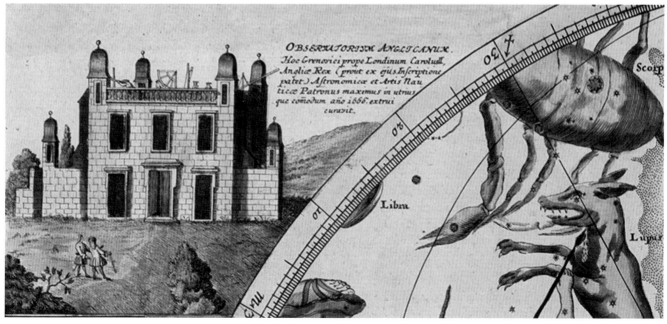

A rare astronomical volvelle by the 'Wheelwright of the Heavens'

125   FERGUSON, James.

The Astronomical Rotula Shewing the Change and Age of the Moon, the Motion of the Sun, Moon and Nodes, with all the Solar and Lunar Eclipses.

London, c.1752. Printed volvelle with five discs, 320mm. diameter. Repairs to outer disc.

A table with five movable discs, allowing the user to determine the positions of the Sun and Moon for every day between 1752 and 1800.

The instrument takes the form of four volvelles over a circular scale, the central volvelle with an engraved face of the sun. These volvelles are designed to show the ecliptic with its twelve signs through which the sun travels in twelve months, to the circle of twelve hours, similar to the dial plate of an early clock, the hour-hand to the sun, and the minute hand to the moon: moving in the ecliptic, the one always overtaking the other at a place farther than it did at their last conjunction. This shows the motions and places of the sun and moon in the ecliptic on each day of the year perpetually and, consequently, the days of all the new and full moons from the years 1752 until 1800.

Despite being born to a poor tenant farmer in Banffshire, Scotland, and having only three months schooling at the age of seven, James Ferguson (1710-76) taught himself enough about astronomy to move to Edinburgh in 1734, where he made orreries and other models, which he used in lectures which he designed to be accessible to the general public. In 1743 he moved to London: he continued to teach, at the Royal Society and as a travelling lecturer. He also had works published, including 'The Use of a New Orrery'; 'Astronomy Explained upon Sir Isaac Newton's Principles' and 'The Young Gentleman and Lady's Astronomy'.

Milburn: Wheelwright of the Heavens: The Life and Work of James Ferguson, FRS.

S/N **16961**